My Happiness Handbook

By Becky Howell

My Happiness Handbook

ISBN: 978-1-7322837-0-1

No part of this book may be used or reproduced in any manner whatsoever without written permission except in the case of brief quotations embodied in critical articles and reviews. For more information go to www.beckyhowell.com.

This handbook is a workshop in a book on happiness. Together, here, we will explore further and farther the concepts that make up happiness, learn how to better define happiness for yourself, and how to bring more happiness into your life by setting yourself up for success. After all, what is happiness if you aren't living it? None of the info here is intended to take the place of professional mental health services or recommendations.

Table of Contents

Finding A Place to Start / 1
    Claim Your Happiness / 4
    How It All Started / 5
    Who This Book Is Intended For / 7
    How We Begin / 12
    How To Use This Handbook / 13

Awareness / 16
    Your Happiness Definition / 18
    Defining Happiness / 22
    Happiness Check In / 28
    Happiness Rescue Remedy / 31
    Your Life Plot / 35
    Looking At Your Life Plot for Trends / 39
    From Life Plot to Life Purpose / 43
    Your Happiness Life Plot / 49
    Summing Awareness Up / 56

Acceptance / 58
    Your Emotional Power / 61
    Learning More About the Mother and Child Roles / 66
    The Solution to Emotional Laboring / 72
    Knowing Your Personality Whys / 76
    Emotional Triggers and Blocks / 78
    One of My Triggers / 79
    Your Self Centers / 81
    Action Steps for Change / 85
    Playing With Blocks / 87

Humans Use Blocks For Protection / 88
Banishing Our Blocks / 91
Matching Our Insides & Our Outsides / 99
Bridging the Gap / 106
Summing Up Acceptance / 111

Forgiveness / 114
A Little On The Word… / 115
A Public Service Announcement on Forgiveness... / 116
Releasing as a Part of Forgiveness / 122
Emotional Reactions / 126
Your Healing Forgiveness Statement / 131
Forgive & Release Exercise / 132
The One Daily Ritual I Keep / 136
Summing Up Forgiveness / 137

Understanding / 139
Transcending Your Past / 142
Releasing Blocks Round 2 / 150
The Why? Game / 155
The What If? Game / 157
Embody Your New Empowered Thought / 158
Important Truths / 160
Summing Up Understanding / 164

Congratulations! / 166

Acknowledgments / 167

References / 168

Additional Support / 172

About The Author / 174

Finding A Place to Start

I live and work at the intersection between science and woo. This unique space is where our inner journey will start.

I began this quest of helping people become happy, healthy and sustainable over a decade ago. It has taken me in many directions, but usually in my safe, hermit-y fashion. I like the quiet of books, gardens, and horses.

While watching *Julie and Julia,* for the billionth time, I realized that, like both Julie and Julia from this wonderful movie, I could also write a book that would help people. I wasn't developing people's palates, and I couldn't make an aspic to save my soul (nasty!), but I knew I had something to offer the world. I could share with more people through a book. Help more people. Inspire more people.

By writing.
Publicly.
Oh.
Uhm...wait!

That also meant that I would have to be visible to more people?!

Possibly made fun of by more people?

Share what I thought (and felt!) with the public?

Errrr… ugh… blech… choke…

I wanted to strangle my own stream of consciousness for even going there. But she wouldn't shut up. Not only that, she was absolutely pitiless. I wasn't able to push the idea away and thought about it (or tried to NOT think about it) all the time.

My own brain was turning on me. Insisting I help others by stripping naked and walking around in public to prove we all have the same wounds, and can still heal. Not only that, while I had always identified with being a writer and a scribbler, I hadn't yet been able to claim the laudable and highly-acclaimed title of…Author. What made me think I could do this now? The doubts and fears kept coming.

A large part of the reason behind my inability to own the title of Author I so desired was directly due to a traumatic incident with my graduate school advisor. She was displeased with my work, and asked me if I had missed school the day they taught writing - in front of the whole department. I was devastated and demoralized, and took what she said as fact. And now, on a whim, I was somehow just supposed to get over that crippling blow to my (wannabe) writer's ego?!

Apparently so.

Which drops us here. Ready to kneel down in fertile earth, considering, musing. Will it support and nurture the most amazing flowers the world has ever seen? Yes.

Claim Your Happiness

I want you to claim this process. Name your story. Write it here. This is (Your Name's) Happiness Handbook.

_____

How It All Started

My formative years were spent at every prison and correctional facility in the state.

What's that you ask? Are you worried about taking healing and self-help advice from a thug or ex-felon? No… I did date a few, but that's another story.

Actually, my mother worked for the Department of Corrections and worked with juvenile and adult rehabilitation programs statewide. She ended up dragging us kids along when grandparents couldn't be cajoled into babysitting. Normal childhood, right? Rather than spend hours on a hard plastic chair, in absolute silence, and smiling innocently every time a secretary suspiciously eyeballed me, I opted to stay in the car a lot of the time. I remembered sitting in that quiet space trying to understand how someone could be so lost, unhappy, and groundless that they ended up in prison. Where was their home? Where was their family? How confusing the path must have been to drop them here away from where they started life.

Eventually, my questions about unhappiness sent me perusing the thick psychology and counseling books in the boxes on the backseat with me. These psychology books were familiar traveling companions. Of course these volumes had diagrams. One of the diagrams that stuck in my head was the model of change used by mental health professionals to explain why change did not happen. It wasn't quite that blunt in the textbook, but I definitely got the impression the authors were glass half-empty people. It sounded like they did not think that change was even possible.

I was outraged and confused. I couldn't believe there wasn't a better way to reach people- to help them get to their life purpose. To help people understand what was needed to be happy. At that moment I started to work on my own system.

Psychology has only relatively recently started to tackle the question of why, and what, makes a person happy. This venerable field of study is just now starting to accept the holistic approach to healing. Previously, only the mind was considered, but what about the rest of the self? Who's looking after the body, spirit, and emotions, as well as the mind? (I call these aspects of self the 'centers'. You'll see me refer to them again and again in the book.)

As someone fascinated by holistic healing, I was frustrated that there was nothing in those thick books to do with the body, spirit, energy or emotions - only the present-tense mind was considered important. I felt that this was deeply and truly wrong, and left so much of a person out. I needed to come up with a more inclusive approach to happiness. That broader approach is what this book is about.

Who This Book Is Intended For

While I truly believe just about everyone would benefit from being happier and, at the very least, becoming familiar with these techniques… the honest truth is, *My Happiness Handbook* isn't going to float everyone's boat. And that's ok. I wrote this specifically for women that have an interest in self-help topics, want to improve their lives, looking for more happiness, and are at least a little curious about what other answers are out there. If terms like self-help, life coaching, mindset, or setting intentions sounds like a goofy foreign language you have never heard before then this handbook might not be for you.

Also, you might have gathered that I am a gardener. I find gratitude and appreciation side-by-side in a row of green beans. From time to time I will rely on gardening anecdotes or metaphors to help me convey an idea. The overall theme of this book is that we GROW ourselves into a beautiful happiness practice. Just like we grow a garden. Over time, and with lots of love and patience.

My view of happiness is holistic. It looks at the state of your entire being at the same time. I see happiness as an emotion, a state of mind, a body experience, and being in spirit. In short, I don't see happiness as limited to the emotional center. Rather, let it be a holistic, encompassing state of being! This book is about bringing all of the parts of you further into the possibilities of your happiness. How can I heal my emotions to be happier? How can I be happier with my body and in my body? How can I clear negative thoughts and self sabotage so that I can be happier in my mind? How can I get closer to God or the Universe so that I can be happier in my spirit?

I touch on some of this in *My Happiness Book* and more thoroughly down in the Awareness chapter of the book you hold in your hands, but basically happiness is about finding the sweet spot between several opposing forces. You find that balance point by learning and growing yourself. That's what this *Happiness Handbook* is about. It is designed to help you to heal and grow into a happier, more complete version of you.

Here in modern times, our lives tend to be segmented. We see a doctor for physical issues, a priest for spiritual, a psychologist for mental, and a pharmacist for emotional issues. It wasn't always this way however. In earlier times, a person was considered and treated as part of a whole being. People were treated physically and spiritually for the same maladie. Things changed when Science and Spirit were separated during the Renaissance. This segmented and split look at a human being is a relatively recent methodology and has been termed Cartesian Doctrine (more info available in the References section).

Evidently Rene Descartes made a backroom deal with the Pope over cadavers. Descartes was allowed to dissect and scientifically observe dead bodies, which had previously been the purview of the church. In return Descartes would concentrate his work on the physical aspects of life, while skirting around, and leaving alone the idea of soul. The soul was the realm of the church and God, and would remain untouchable.

This approach has carried through 'til today. We are just now starting to recover from this and regain a holistic view of life.

The definition of holistic (that I lifted straight from *Merriam Webster*) is: relating to or concerned with wholes or with complete systems rather than with the analysis of, treatment of, or dissection into parts. Holistic medicine attempts to treat both the mind and the body. However, my issue is that is still not holistic. We are minds, bodies, spirits, and emotions - bound together by energy - grounded in earth, and sharing this life experience. *That* is a holistic view, and that is the definition I refer to throughout this workbook.

This holistic view is important to share because this reductionist way of living does not work! You know, I wanted to skate around being this whole thing. I didn't want to be bold. I wanted to remain on the side of ambiguity regarding the whole Western approach to health. My aim in the first, second, and third draft of this paragraph was to let you, the reader, and owner of your story, come to your own conclusions. But...well, I can't! My truth, that I need to share, is that you can't find health or happiness by dissecting apart your self-centers (mind-body-spirit-emotions) and giving them to byzantine establishments entrenched in dusty dogma - devoid of compassion or authenticity.

We have gotten to this place of parceling out - us! If we are having issues with how we look, we try a diet pill or surgery, or merely loathe our bodies. If we are anxious and unhappy, we try the newest anti-anxiety med, or see a shrink who doesn't empathize and keeps doling out meds. If we are feeling empty and unfulfilled, yep, another pill prescribed by another white coat. And all this is not to say that medicinal help is to be looked down upon, or eschewed. But, it needs to come from a true place of healing where someone is appreciating that we are a whole being, and a lot more than our aching singular part.

Back to my gardening metaphor, what crops can you grow without dynamic, healthy soil? What happiness can be grown on ground with no topsoil, no microbes or living structure?? Soil that has been stripped of all its life isn't healthy and will struggle to produce anything at all. A bigger picture is that a flower pot needs water, sunlight, nutrients, and symbiotic microorganisms. All of these elements together support a holistic life. Missing any one of these things makes the soil insufficient for growth.

The futility baked into those psychology textbooks, the resignation of the social workers, and the depression displayed by the incarcerated did not allow for the ability to create happiness. The segmented view of psychology doesn't often resolve the past. It certainly isn't holistic, and it doesn't seem to be a safe bet for the incarcerated. It feels like setting people up to fail. How are people supposed to heal without a holistic approach? I don't think ten years on the couch rehashing the same conversation is the answer either. I wanted more for the world. So I created a process to guide people through becoming happier from the inside out.

In this handbook, I'll take you through my four-step process for true, holistic change in order to bring more happiness in to your life:

1. Awareness
2. Acceptance
3. Forgiveness
4. Understanding

How We Begin

My programs always start with awareness because creating change requires an understanding of where we are at any given moment - and - knowing where we have been. This allows us to see our Why, and plan out the How of our change. The Why is the primary reason behind our actions and the How is our individual path to creating change. Together these make up our map and allows us to journey forward through change, instead of travelling in circles.

Then we will move into accepting our truth(s). This section of the handbook can be challenging for people. Truth is not always easy to see. It is easy to deny, or shift the responsibility of our actions or emotions to another person or situation. However, being able to boldly claim your truth is incredibly liberating. I spent a good chunk of years getting really good at denying my pesky emotions, my truths, and burying them inside. But true health and happiness are found in accepting what **is** as truth, as YOUR truth.

The next step is working through forgiveness. To create our own happiness we must forgive others, let go of situations, and forgive ourselves. This helps trauma pass through us, rather than stay and make us sick. I define trauma as a negative memory trapped inside your mind and body. Holding low vibration emotions and trauma inside of you can make you sick. By allowing these emotions awareness and space, and then to flow through you, rather than trying not to look at it, helps you keep reaching toward your highest health and happiness.

And lastly, understanding is a space where you will bring together a little science, a little woo, and your learning from the entire handbook! This final section will allow you a place to record how you approach the world, and happiness, and combine it with all of your new learning to create something astoundingly perfect for your holistic self.

How To Use This Handbook

My Happiness Handbook is intended to further the journey hinted at in *My Happiness Book*. To be clear, my first book is not a requirement to get the full weight of this one. Both are more than capable of standing alone, but they do play nicely together.

Let's dive deep, get real, roll around in our own earthly shortcomings, and plant seeds that will grow into beauties. Together, you and I will create from scratch, a beautiful, consciously created, thriving happiness practice.

Each of us is at a different stage in our life journey. Many can be found brazenly planning on a forty acre garden the first year. They have big plans for their happiness and are excited about their new creations. While others are more comfortable quietly designing a window box, or buying a colorful hanging basket to enjoy.

If you've already read *My Happiness Book*, you may have easily answered all the questions I posed there, duly noting and outlining it. Maybe you sped right past the questions, devouring the lush illustrations and allowing the words to simmer quietly in the back of your mind. The beauty of *My Happiness Book* is that any reaction you had to it was absolutely correct!

This handbook, in comparison, will guide you through some of the deeper ideas that help to create your happiness. Not in a haphazard way, but with intention and purpose. I recommend walking through these questions and thought-starters in the order presented. There are times when it might seem that I am leading you in circles, that we aren't going in a direct line, or that it feels a little out of order like going down parallel train tracks… I beg your patience during these moments. There is a reason for the madness. In one of my lives I taught university classes. I realized then how much the person asking the question can influence a student's answer. I've found we can get to more powerful answers if I sometimes explain why after you've done the work. I don't want to influence your answers. This is intentional. Just play along. Your results will be better. I promise!

I will be introducing some powerful questions, meditations, thoughts, personal stories, and resources to help you explore what happiness really means to you. I have tried to include space for your own thoughts and revelations, but if you tend to write in a large hand (or in my case have a practically illegible scrawl), or are reading this digitally perhaps a separate journal would be beneficial.

I have written this book so that it feels like I am right there with you in a coaching call, or at one of my workshops. I've included *My Thoughts on This* sections that have extra insight scattered throughout to ensure I am making the point that I am intending. The *Watch Out Woo* sections are where I bring in some of my own spirituality. Feel to skip them if they don't serve. It is important to work through this in an open frame of mind with lots of curiosity. Sometimes when we dig deep, our mind interprets this as an attack, and will turn to self-sabotage for protection. No need for that here, our desire and intention is to bring more happiness into your life.

My highest hope for all of my books is that you find them liberating, hopeful, and that they facilitate change for you. That is my biggest compliment and highest goal.

Get your pens, pencils, or coloring markers. Will you use a journal to neatly keep track of your thoughts, or are you going to squeeze your answers in here, and fill up the pages within?

Ready?

Let's go!

Awareness

Introduction

Awareness is the first step to generating any change needed to bring more happiness into your life. Awareness is like clearing off the weeds so you can see what's actually there in the ground underneath. It leads you to your next step. You have to become aware of where you are now, in order to get to where you want to be.

You can gain greater awareness in your life by questioning, probing, uncovering your typical reactions to situations, thoughts, and feelings. Sometimes this work can feel difficult. It's not easy to see ourselves with more clarity. It is guaranteed that there will be some things in there you won't like. But this awareness work is oh-so-necessary for shedding beliefs that don't work for you any longer. These old beliefs, thoughts, and feelings are what keep you stuck and unhappy.

This is why I liken this to clearing the sod. We don't know what we have to work with until we unbury it. We must see it. Awareness strips away what is cloaking the surface so we can see what is really there. So that we can approach our happiness awareness from Who we are and How we got there.

For any big breakthrough, awareness is that moment of neural and emotional connection. The Ah-Hah, or Eureka moment! That moment when Helen Keller understood 'w-a-t-e-r' for the first time. This is one of the most primal moments in human history, all centered around two women. Can you imagine the magnitude of incredible awareness Helen experienced in that moment?

Water. Understanding how to communicate in one simple word.

And, for Helen Keller a galaxy of awareness opened. That one word led to greater expression, finding her purpose, and learning what made her happy. This magical experience isn't just for Ms Keller. Transformation and greater levels of happiness all starts with awareness for you as well.

Acceptance is seeing the truth. Forgiveness is about healing those truths. Understanding is about weaving the truths into your being so that your life is stronger and a thing of joy.

In this section on awareness we will decode your happiness language so you understand clearly what you want your happy life to look like. We will setup your Happiness Gradient and create a happiness rescue plan. My Happiness Rescue Remedy is incredibly helpful in times when you are feeling down. We will also take a walk back through your Life Plot and Happiness Plot so that you can have greater awareness about how you got to where you are on your happiness journey. You will also get to discover your Life Purpose. That alone is incredibly valuable and will serve you over and over. I'll also introduce two different philosophies of being happy and how to integrate both into your world. So much fun and exploration into your awareness await!

Your Happiness Definition

I've found two different philosophical ideas that have helped to shape and define my work around happiness. Of course, each person must have their own definition of what happiness is to them but these are a good place to start exploring. This is because creating happiness is such an individual process. No two people create or envisage happiness in quite the same way. In deciding on your own definition, you will become more aware of what actually creates happiness for you - both internally and externally - and how to use both approaches consciously to create even more happiness.

One philosophy (introduced by Aristotle) of an internal component of happiness is knowing your life purpose. Aristotle believed that if you understand your purpose it can lead to greater levels of fulfillment and joy. How does that philosophy sit with you? Why you are here on this planet? What makes your life meaningful? Understanding and living in your purpose is the basis for a kind of happiness mentioned in *My Happiness Book*, termed **Eudaimonic Happiness.**

In contrast to looking at your internal happiness, there is a philosophy that deals with your external happiness. This view involves seeking pleasurable life experiences in order to create joy and fulfillment. Experiences like vacations, romantic relationships, or creating success at work. We call this external side of your happiness definition, **Hedonistic Happiness**.

Let's bring these two ideas of internal and external happiness together to create your definition. You can think of your own personal definition of happiness as a set of sliding scales that you get to set for yourself. Tweak this one to the left. Move that one all the way to the right. Touch that one a little… no more… no too much… there! Your happiness definition is a continuous adjustment of what you hold valuable internally and externally.

My Thoughts on This:

Not only do you want to define your happiness specifically, it is also important to grow your internal resilience to the ups and downs of life. Throughout the course of your life, you will inevitably be faced with negative situations and energy in life. It's likely you already have, and you know what I'm talking about. The more resilient you are, the more able you will be to bounce back when life sends you events or people that knock you off your center. It is even possible to get to a place where regardless of what else is going on around you, you can rely on your internal state of being, instead of feeling knocked around by life. That's what I call happiness!

Because let's face it... there is a whole buncha crazy going on right now. Having a strong and resilient state of internal happiness is going to be CRUCIAL to thriving in a world that is starting to resemble a giant dumpster fire.

Like I said, part of having a strong happiness game is having a working vocabulary. Let's establish a definition for you. When you have a proper definition of what happiness means to you, you have created your new North. When you have a strong guiding principle, you can more easily align to that feeling and definition. The awareness of the language you use around your happiness is important. The words you have available to express yourself can be limiting! By widening your happiness vocab to include the words you actually mean, you will be better served to be able to discuss your happiness, and to voice your wants, dreams, needs and expectations.

Look at it this way. Imagine going into a beautiful garden center. Flowering pots. Dripping ferns. Artful displays with water fountains. But you are only allowed to speak words that start with the letter A. Unless you only want to know where the Agapanthus and Alyssum are... then you are in trouble. Who wants a garden filled with plants that only start with the letter A? Although I love Alyssum, I don't want that to be the only flower in my garden. That would not make me happy.

How many times have you felt frustrated and defeated when you didn't know the right words, at the right time for an argument. Or somehow felt unable to describe what you were feeling to someone else? Becoming aware of the words that work for you, and describe your happiness is the answer!

Defining Happiness

When you think of the word, *happy* what other words come to mind? Feel free to go to Thesaurus.com, type in the word *happy* and pick as many words you like.

_____

_____

_____

Our mind associates words together with emotions. Words can definitely remind you of positive or negative experiences. These experiences are held as memories and are layered with emotion. What happens when you hear the word *sex*, or *rain*? I bet it brings up emotions for you. It is important to set yourself up for true happiness by using words and phrases that mean positive things to you.

What are a few words that you associate with happiness?

_____

_____

_____

One of my biggest pet peeves about words, is that the denotations (literal or primary definition of a word) and connotations (non-literal, non-primary definition of a word) that people place on concepts, based on their own unique experiences, are not considered to have any influence on a person's emotional wellbeing. We all have history, and just as some songs can really grate and cause a negative reaction, so can words.

For example, my association with the word *try* has a completely different feel than most people's. *Try* has a **denotation** of making an attempt or an effort to do something. But some people's **connotation** of the word, *try* is a nod to the infamous Yoda quote, "Do or do not, there is no try." So for many people *try* means a half-hearted attempt. Wow, that irks me. When I use the word *try*, I use it in the same way my grandparents did. I use it as a noun. Saying someone has tremendous *try* is an accolade. Don't tell me not to use *try*!

So our words matter, especially when it comes to building an emotional framework that has been previously missing in our lives - like happiness, or joy, or love. It is actually pretty common for people to feel disenfranchised and left out when they hear the word *happy*. You might not identify with the word *happy* because it reminds you of dumb blonde stereotypes, or that scene in *When Harry Met Sally* ('Ok, yes, basically I am a happy person and I don't see what's wrong with that'), or something else embedded in your brain. Let's make sure to get some words that DO work for you.

Use FIVE of your *happy* words from the exercises above to create a sliding scale of happiness. I encourage you to establish degrees of happiness from most mellow to most vibrant. (My sliding scale would be: content, calm, excited, fulfilled, and joyous.) What five words make up your **Happiness Gradient**?

_____

_____

_____

Now, look up the denotation of each word and include your own connotation after. Remember, a denotation is the primary meaning of a word. The connotation is the feeling, or symbolism of a word. Why both? This goes back to getting our gardening area free and clear of weeds, just like our minds. We don't want to sabotage ourselves right from the start and allow weeds to take over the garden by accidentally leaving some roots behind. Sometimes we have associations with words that are different than their actual meaning, or our definitions might be muddied. This exercise gives you a chance to be crystal clear with your word choice. Emotions can be tricky enough to describe without tripping over the vocab.

_____

_____

_____

_____

_____

_____

_____

Watch Out Woo

Why are these definitions so important? Because if you don't know, with a good deal of clarity, what to ask the Universe for how can you possibly create it? If you go into a luscious, blooming gardening center and expect to get answers on why your roses are dying, but you don't know why or how to describe white mildew or black spot, how can the nursery expert possibly give you a satisfactory answer?

In the same way, how can you possibly create happiness in your life, if you have no idea how to talk about it? This is exactly how it works with the Universe. If you don't have the awareness of your happiness vocabulary to order up the happiness you want, how can you call it in?

My Thoughts on This:
Don't believe me on the power of thought? I got exercises for you in the Understanding section that will blow your mind and give you an inkling of what you are actually capable of!

During a typical day, how many times do you experience each of the words on your Happiness Gradient? Answer honestly. Whatever the answer, it's okay. We are establishing a benchmark of where you are now so that we have something to compare and contrast with later.

_____

_____

_____

What activities do you participate in that help you access happy emotions? List as many as you can.

_____

_____

_____

How many times do you experience your highest happy emotion on a weekly basis?

_____

On a monthly basis?_____

Now that we have kicked this around a little bit, I'm going to ask again because I want your deeper answer here. It is easy to answer a question like this with an activity that is right in front of your face (TV, knitting, and playing with your pets... anyone?) This is your second chance to dig a little deeper and see what else comes up.

What brings you your highest expression of happiness? This could be hedonistic (pleasurable experiences) or eudaemonic expressions of happiness (life purpose). Could be anything from family, to chocolate, to volunteering at a soup kitchen, to finishing a marathon... pick 4 things, or areas in your life that bring out your highest happiness.

___

___

___

___

How can you bring these into your life on a regular basis? These are your Happiness Goals. These are instances you want to enrich your life, and yield more happiness. Spend some time here brainstorming 1-2 happiness goals for the next week. How might you do at least one of these activities more often?

___

___

___

We're not finished yet. Pause here, grab your phone or planner and put a date or find a time to add these to your calendar. We all know that if something isn't scheduled, it ain't gonna happen! Where are you making time for your own happiness? Now is the time.

Happiness Check In

Now that you are becoming more aware of your happiness, and how you define it, you can use that awareness on a daily basis. It is important to be aware of how you are doing from moment to moment. How do you feel about doing whatever is happening in front of you? It's time to check in. Are you happy? Stressed? Calm? Listen to what your inner voice is telling you. It's an important part of this awareness process.

(IMPORTANT Disclaimer: this does not mean you should quit or run away from everything that is not making you ecstatic. There is a balance to life. This book is about creating your balance.)

My Thoughts on This:
Happiness Check Ins are something I do frequently for myself. I go to talk about them in the 'Hack Your Happiness' podcast with the lovely Michelle Reinhardt.(http://michellereinhardt.com.au/hack-your-happiness-for-unlimited-abundance-with-becky-howell) Approaching life through the balance point of happiness, is a quick and easy

way to get a handle on what is going on for you, how you are doing, what could be better in your life, and where you need to put focus so you can be happier.

How do you feel right now? What is happening for you? How are things going in your life? Would you consider yourself a happy person?

Write until you feel complete.

_____

_____

_____

Are you content with how much time you spend pursuing external activities that make you happy?

_____

_____

_____

Is there room for tweaking here? Or are you satisfied with how you are spending your time, in general?

_____

_____

_____

Do your happiness activities bring you joy and put you back in balance?

___

Don't be surprised if you want more time and space to pursue these happiness activities. It is common to want more of your life to be focused on the activities that bring you joy. If you are not practiced at consciously balancing your work and life activities, it can be easy to spend all of your available time on working. Sound like anyone you know? You and I are here together to bring in the balance.

My Thoughts on This:
Here is a powerful Happiness Check In result from my own work from when I first started coaching. After using holistic methods to coach people through their anxiety, I became the 'Anti-Anxiety Coach.' My days were full of sessions and my clients were seeing results. However, during one of my own Happiness Check-Ins, I realized I didn't want to continue on the same path. It was a high-touch, constant-access program and it was burning me out. I was suffering from anxiety myself and didn't appreciate the irony. I was not happy with that kind of work-life balance. I realized that I could achieve higher levels of happiness for myself, and preserve my sanity, by shifting the focus of my work. I am so much happier!

My personal suggestion is to do this weekly, at the outside, every month. This can make a great meditation to add to your wellness practice!

Happiness Rescue Remedy

Now that you are checking in on your happiness more often, you will be more aware of when you aren't happy. It isn't easy to keep a hawk eye on your emotional fitness while just trying to make it through the day. All too often we end up cranky or down. This is where my Happiness Rescue Remedy comes into play.

We can be cruising along doing well on our happiness journey, and then something happens. We stumble, have a bad day, or get some not-so-great news, and BAM, we are down in the dumps. I used to feel like I was drowning, just stuck and depressed. Like nothing would ever bring me out. Like I could sleep forever or watch Netflix for eternity. It felt so difficult to create happiness. Those ups and downs from life really affected me.

The trick here is to realize when you are down. Thinking of positive things when you feel down can be difficult. Especially if you are feeling emotional. It is just too much of a disconnect between where you are in that upset state to shift directly into your happiness. When you are upset, you have to slowly work your way back to calm, and then relaxed ease, then back into happiness. The next time you are feeling good, you are going to create a list of activities that walk you back from upset and into your higher energy. This will become your Happiness Rescue Remedy!

You didn't know it at the time, but you have already done part of the work. Pick the happiness activities that you listed above. Start with the activities that help you to be emotionally calm and easy. Then escalate up to the activities that take you to those bigger, happier emotions. Write the emotion you are aiming for and the chosen activity for your Happiness Rescue Remedy. Please remember, do this exercise when you are feeling in a good mood!

1. _____
   (less involved, calmer)
2. _____
3. _____
4. _____
5. _____
   (more involved, higher emotion)

There will be times when you don't have to use all of your happiness activities, there will be times that you do. But having this figured out as a plan ahead of time is invaluable.

For the big money, I will give you the other piece of this. After you have used this about 5 times CHANGE IT. Your Happiness Rescue Remedy needs to feel fresh, fun and engaging. Nothing done in a bored frame of mind is going to elevate your energy. So keep planning ahead to develop and strengthen your happiness game!

I'll share my plan so you can see what this looks like. Remember I said this needs to be changed over time? Mine looks like this for the moment:

1. Going for a run
2. Practicing my dulcimer,
3. Digging out my paints and doing watercolor
4. Gardening
5. Planning and going for a weekend away.

It is all too easy to start relying on others for your Happiness Rescue Remedy. Please resist this temptation! It really is best if these are self-starter activities. Then if your peeps don't wanna play ball when you do, you don't end up screwed and feeling worse than ever. Being able to have a self-sustainable happiness practice is bigtime important. Your emotional state isn't anyone else's responsibility but yours. Learning how to have emotional resilience in this life will put you so far ahead of the game you won't believe how much easier the mechanics of living becomes. We'll talk more about this idea of taking care of your own happiness in the acceptance section, so stay tuned.

We started on the external - hedonistic side of your happiness. You now have clarity around your happiness language, and some of the activities that bring more happiness into your life. Now I want to shift to the internal.

The next important awareness to creating happiness is getting clear on your whys. What you will discover are some of your big Whys. Not the little whys like, why go to the grocery store; why won't the light come on; why isn't my favorite show still on the History Channel? This is about your BIG Whys. Why do you wake up in the morning? Why are you here? Why do you react in the way you do? Why are you having a hard time forgiving? Why is your relationship struggling?

Most people work to be happy, but end up frustrated at their inability to create lasting happiness. If you are like most people, you feel like you take two steps forward, but end up sliding into old reactionary patterns and behaviors. If that sounds like you, then great! This is the section for you.

I have found that most people need to know the why to a behavior in order to change it. It is having a clear understanding of the why we do something, and why it isn't working for us that gives us the impetus to change. Why is one of the great change initiators.

Asking yourself Why, can be a powerful game to play. We'll be playing the Why Game later on in the book. I was able to articulate big frustrations in my life through the Why Game and numerous clients have fallen in love with this simple technique as well. Some of the heavy hitters that were answered thru the Why Game include: Why am I sick so often? Why do I feel burned out with such frequency? (Answer: I don't always have the best work-play balance. I tend to go hell-for-leather until I collapse.)

So by bringing in the Why Game and the understanding of Life Plots (see below), I was able to see the rest of the story. The way I was approaching work was a carbon copy of how my mother approached work. It is stamped in my psyche that if you aren't working balls to the wall, you aren't doing enough. I had picked up the belief that if you aren't exhausted, you didn't work hard enough. And that you didn't get to take off or recover until you were actually sick. Isn't that crazy? So by reminding myself in the thick of it that it is ok to take breaks, I can create my OWN work-play balance. I can keep my wellness on an even keel.

Your Life Plot

As mentioned above, I wanted to share another of the techniques I teach that help my clients get to their big whys. You do this by first writing an overview of your life. You'll take that overview and describe the plot or story of your life as if you were the hero/ine of your own movie. Because you are. I call this your **Life Plot**. I'll show you how to do it more specifically in a moment.

Writing out your Life Plot is an effective way to get an overview of your past. It's a great way to see what went into the making of you, and why you, the main character, ends up falling for the same kinda guy over-and-over again, or hates that office job but stays anyway. Or maybe why you feel strongly called to be a musician.

Have you ever planted a bush, after a shrub, after a tree in the same spot - only to have them all die? You keep trying different things, but none of them seem to work to produce a thriving plant? You need to dig deep and see what's under the roots that is causing the surface behavior. Being able to work through a Life Plot is like getting your set of special instructions on how much sun each plant needs.

Your Life Plot will include the following:

- What have you done, accomplished or avoided?
- What experiences have you had that really stick out in your memory?
- What have you learned, good or bad?
- What have you observed that are recurring themes in your life?
- What are the trends and patterns you see?

Tips to help you write the most effective Life Plot:

- When you start writing your Life Plot, aim for a middle voice. You don't have to be super-positive, but don't write from the pit of despair either. I recommend writing as an observer, in the third person. Perhaps even orated in a cheesy announcer's voice (I won't tell;)

- The point here is to help you see your life from another angle. Pretend someone else is writing this as a biography of your life.
- I organized my Life Plot based on my education but if something else makes more sense for you (different families, different states you lived in, different phases you went through) use that instead.

Mine reads like this:

Becky always been interested in healthy living and alternative therapies. Even as a small girl she would often make medicines in a rotted stump with leaves, pinecones, mushrooms, and rainwater. She has always loved animals, nature, and books from the time she was young. Becky has always been stubborn, independent, and realized at an early age that she wanted to do things her own way. She never wanted to be conventional or mainstream, and never accepted an answer without getting the why *behind it. This didn't always endear her to the adults in her life. In high school Becky wanted to be a large animal vet or author. In school plays, she preferred working behind the scenes as a stage manager, rather than being out front and visible, which made her incredibly anxious.*

She continued to explore herb lore, Reiki, aromatherapy, and other alternative therapies. College saw her explode out and take as many courses as she could squeeze in, all of that knowledge in such a free setting made her giddy. The Navy, on the other hand, was a total nightmare, and taught her she preferred living on land. She hated form and structure and rigidity, not to mention a boss. Graduate school was spent learning how to organize, think critically, and feel the need to make the world a better place. During grad school Becky became very sick, and was gifted time to heal and think. She awakened to the limitations of Western medicine and Western style counseling and knew people were missing the holistic approach to healing.

Now it's your turn. Write out your Life Plot. Ask yourself the following:

- What have you done, accomplished or avoided?
- Where have you gone that really sticks out in your memory?
- What have you learned, good or bad?
- What have you observed that are recurring themes in your life?
- What are the trends and patterns you see?

First make notes about the answers, and then write it out in story form from the third person perspective, as I did mine. I've given you some space below, but given the nature of the exercise, feel free to use more.

Looking At Your Life Plot for Trends

When you sift through your life in this way, you'll start to see patterns clearly. It is awareness that can help us to release old patterns, and take the first step in consciously creating what we want in our lives - more happiness!

Looking through my Life Plot, you see a need for change and education. A love of all things to do with nature. An independent spirit. A drive to help, especially in a holistic fashion. I have been tweaking my businesses to get closer and closer to my highest happiness every year. I am self-employed, and all of my work is centered on helping others find their own health and wellness. I continue to invest in my education and life experiences.

Watch Out Woo

Personally I believe that there is a lesson and pattern behind most of what has happened/will happen in our lives. It can be tough to see this pattern as it is being knitted, but if you look back along your life, the pattern is more obvious. It is a deeply spiritual process to know and believe that our lives aren't a collection of coincidences and mistakes. Seeing the pattern in my chaos helped me step closer to the big U.

What do you see looking into your own Life Plot? What patterns emerge for you? It reminds me of the difference between living an event and reading about it in a history book. In the moment everything seems chaotic, layered, with no pattern. It is hard to to get perspective, interpret, and see meaning in the swirl. But with a little perspective, and some time, things can become more clear. What patterns are you seeing in your Life Plot?

___

My Thoughts on This:
Don't worry if you find these activities and questions frustrating, or weird. I'm asking you to use different neural pathways, and different ways of thinking about your life. Just do your best. You can't fail. Part of this awareness section is about warming up your intuitive mus-

cles. Everyone has intuition, but some of us need to limber it up and strengthen it.

Looking back through your LIfe Plot, can you see any patterns in the experiences in your life that have brought you happiness?

___

___

___

___

___

___

___

___

My Thoughts on This:
Isn't this exciting? Seeing your life from a different perspective? When we live it, everything can seem disjointed. But by looking at your Life Plot, you can see that there is a method to the madness. We each are outfitted with a large backpack at birth. Our whole life we are stuffing lessons, experiences, neuroses, blocks, memories, everything into that bag. If you were to dump it out on the floor, it would be a mess! No patterns, no rhyme or reason, just a heap of confusion. However,

when you sort it out, organize it, and then reconstruct the pieces, you will see similar circumstances, echos of the same reactions, a guiding thread leading you toward something. Knowing how to interpret the mess will give you the awareness to make better choices for more happiness.

You've now seen your life from a different perspective. You've also seen clearly what patterns have emerged for you throughout your life, including what's helped you create more happiness. It can be interesting to see for the first time. What were your biggest takeaways from this exercise? What did you learn about yourself?

_____

_____

_____

_____

_____

_____

From Life Plot to Life Purpose

Now, let's move from your Life Plot to your Life Purpose. We are going to keep this simple. You are going to take your

Life Plot and boil it down to one sentence. This is your Life Purpose. As I mentioned before, understanding your raison d'etre is critical for having a sustainable happiness practice. Your happiness is a balance between pleasurable experiences (hedonistic happiness) and fulfilling our life purpose (eudaimonic happiness). Understanding your Life Purpose is an essential step on the path to creating that balance.

Experiment with summing up your Life Plot below into one sentence here. You may need more space.

_____

_____

_____

_____

_____

_____

My Thoughts on This:
A fun tool for this exercise is to take your whole paragraph from above and type it into a WordCloud generator (one of my faves: https://worditout.com/word-cloud/create) to see what words show up most frequently in your Life Plot. What words pop out at you? What are you saying over and over? What stood out to me was the word 'school', words to do with nature, healing, and health. What about you?

Now, let's take your summary sentence, and structure it into your Life Purpose Statement this way:

I am here to _____(verb: help, grow, teach, lead, facilitate, mentor, build, grow, protect, etc)

_____(noun: species, specific group of people, area, age, idea etc)

_____(verb: action, do what)

_____(preposition: by, because of, due to, with my)

_____(phrase that takes into account your life plot, what is unique, different, special to you.)

Here is my Life Purpose Statement as an example.

I am here to help and lead humans and horses to their greatest holistic health and potential.

Getting a feel for what this should look like? Now it's your turn. Given the structure I just gave you, use this space to write out your Life Purpose Statement.

_____

_____

_____

My Thoughts on This:
My editor and I argued over this point. I feel like our purpose can sound audacious and braggy the first time you own it. My editor on the other hand, wanted me to model bold behavior and claim it with no apology. Therefore, we will settle it by saying that our Spirits are infinite. And that is truth.

You are not simply a list of chores, or a culmination of your resume, or a caregiver to your family. Everyone has something big to do in this life. And when I say big, I mean bigger than your immediate family. You are a perfect amalgamation of personality, situation, environment, and life experience that culminates in you helping to create a positive exchange in the world. Whatever change seems meaningful and exciting to you. That is what your Life Purpose represents.

The phrasing of your Life Purpose should be a little vague so that it will fit all stages of your life, but it needs to pack power and energy. When you say your purpose out loud, you want it to feel like a mic drop when you are finished. You should be smiling and feel strong. If it's the right Life Purpose for you, it should feel in alignment with who you are on a deep level.

My Thoughts on This:
This Life Purpose exercise can be hard for many of us to do! We are taught to be smaller, to not want big things, to be humble, to love our

families above all else. So if this is your first exposure to thinking bigger, it is time to dare to dream!

Watch Out Woo

I personally believe that our spirits agreed to our purpose and lessons before being sent for a rebirth. We just don't know how we will receive them. So the sooner we make the conscious choice to engage with why we are here, the better chance we have of creating real and lasting happiness!

Why am I making you do all this, answer all these questions, think about all these ideas? One of my favorite authors and thinkers, Don Miguel Ruiz asks in *The Voice of Knowledge*, "How do we live our life? This is our art, the art of living. With our power of creation, we express the force of life in everything we say, everything we feel, everything we do. But there are two kinds of artists, the ones who create their story without awareness and the ones who recover awareness and create their story with truth and love." I ask these questions, and make you think about these things because it is my goal to give you awareness so that you can consciously create your story with truth, love, and happiness.

My Thoughts on This:
The first time you write out your life purpose it might feel silly or weird. What happens if it is real? Does your Life Purpose feel too big to claim? Too out there? I have a fun exercise that will help you play

with your new ideas, called My What If Game. It is waiting for you in the Understanding section.

Ok, so now you have a very simple, but powerful Life Purpose. Understanding why you are here is a huge part of your happiness journey. This type of eudaimonic happiness suggests that knowing our Why, our Purpose, our raison d'être, *and working toward it* allows us to feel truly happy and self actualized.

What did looking at your Life Purpose show you about yourself?

_____

_____

_____

Please understand that these aren't just fluffy self-awarenesses here. Your Life Plot and Life Purpose are useful tools for your life. Having awareness about yourself, and what brings you joy, on a deeper level can help you to make tough decisions in a more aligned way.

Knowing these things about myself makes it easier to make tricky decisions about my next step. Is this next project a good thing for me to do? I'll look to see if it is in alignment with my Life Purpose. Should I move to an apartment in the middle of LA, or an isolated cabin atop a mountain?

The answer to both is probably not. They make living my purpose harder. Decision made.

Where have you had difficulty making decisions in the past? Jot down any thoughts about how knowing your Life Plot and Life Purpose may have helped you to make that decision more easily.

_____

_____

_____

Your Happiness Life Plot

Time to take your Life Plot, and do the big cheese! Let's take those same principles we used to create your Life Plot and apply them to sketching out your **Happiness Life Plot.** Your Happiness Life Plot sums up your life in a chronological fashion just like we did for your Life Plot, but focuses the work specifically on your happiness. Here are some questions to get you started:

- What messages have you received about happiness?
- How did others around you relate to happiness?
- What were the lessons (good or bad) that you picked up around happiness?

- As you read your Life Plot that you created earlier, does it feel happy to you?

Write out the answers to the questions here.

___

___

___

___

___

___

Now take those answers and form them into your Happiness Life Plot here. If writing it in the first person feels tricky, try writing it in the third person like we did before.

___

___

___

___

___

___

Here is an example of my Happiness Life Plot:

I was always expected to be happy, and make those around me happy, even though most of the surrounding adults were not. I learned to fake my happiness early. Yet, I was chastised frequently for being too loud when I was just being authentically happy. I also learned that no one wanted to play with the sad kid, which either made me angry, more sad, or again I just faked being happy. High school became about setting my sights on escaping, and to do so, achieving perfection.

Perfectionism was a way for me to control emotions, expectations, and outcomes. The Navy and Grad school taught me to build a protective shell around my emotions, because experiencing them, or even showing them was dangerous. I became deathly ill during grad school, looking back I know this was a side-effect of the emotional and energetic strain I was under. The years I needed to physically heal gave me time to start putting together my emotional wellness.

My father had a bit of cruel streak when he was up, but was frequently depressed. My mother expressed happiness when she was poking fun at others. One set of grandparents were never happy and complained about everything. The other set had the approach that life was about work, and happiness was frivolous. This is the awareness part of my story.

I also want to show what the rest of the story looks like. It is important to include a bit about acceptance, forgiveness, and understanding here. It is all too easy to start the blame game when looking at any of your Life Plots. That energy will not serve our purposes here.

My grandparents were Depression babies. One of my Great-Greats drove a covered wagon from Tennessee as child. My grandfather worked 3 jobs (19hrs a day for 15yrs) and suffered from a host of physical issues. My father's father was an alcoholic and was abused as a child. These are pieces of information to hold WITH the first part of my Happiness Life Plot. The things that did, or didn't happen to me did not occur in a vacuum. No one's history does. These things have been going on for generations. Centuries. Eons.

This is awareness and acceptance. Forgiveness is letting all that go. It is my work to release my miserly grip on what my family did or didn't do so that I can stop carrying it with me, and abusing myself with it. Understanding is sifting through this genetic and cultural inheritance, consciously creating what I want for my journey, and realizing how limitless we actually are.

When you look at my Happiness Life Plot, you can see that I was experiencing emotional dissonance from a very young age. Emotional dissonance is when the emotion that you exhibit is different from what you are actually feeling. I took on the role of being responsible for other people's happiness without having the tools to accomplish my own. Because I felt that no one could receive me for my own true emotional state, I started to distrust my own happiness, and my emotions in general. Especially when happiness wasn't being mirrored or expressed around me.

The problem is even though we might not have the right tools to build happiness for ourselves, we still go out and attempt to fill that emotional void. We want to be happy. But if we don't know how, how do we actually do it? I tried to fill the happiness void in myself with men, wine, food, the complete absence of food, driving too fast, driving too far, busyness, extreme fitness, and depression. Let me save y'all some time... none of those things worked either.

I had to get so real with this stuff in order to save myself that I thought I should share this journey in case others were on it too. You need to know the Whys. You need to know how you got to this point and what were the contributing factors. Your Happiness Life Plot will help you do that.

So, look back through your Happiness Life Plot. What patterns do you see? What were your contributing factors?

_____

_____

_____

Were you happy as a child? _____

Teen? _____

What about now?

___

___

___

How did you express being happy while you were growing up?

___

___

___

When did you feel happiest?

___

___

___

Did you ever struggle with feeling happy?

___

___

___

Who did, or didn't teach you the most about happiness?

___

___

___

What are your biggest takeaways from the Happiness Life Plot exercise?

___

___

___

What are your biggest awarenesses around your own happiness so far?

___

___

___

Summing Awareness Up

Congratulations on sticking it through and getting some incredible awareness around where you stand in terms of your own happiness! You have quite a blueprint for creating your own special blend of happiness moving forward. From the inside-out. Yay!!! You also have some pretty great practices for getting you back to happiness when you are feeling down. Great work.

Here is a recap of what you've become aware of around your happiness:

- You established your happiness language and your emotion words (and why they are different) so that you can lay out your goals and what you want to experience.
- You have your happiness gradient and know the activities that link your experience with an action. I call this your Rescue Remedy for Happiness and it is very helpful for getting back into your happiness practice!
- You are able to see the importance of being able to actively express what you want now as your Happiness Goals.
- You understand that not having the correct language around happiness leads to more UN-happiness.
- You have sketched out your Life Plot and explored the

patterns of your life that have brought you what you wanted, or not.
- You have used the Life Plot to decode your life purpose - another essential step in your happiness journey.
- You are aware of both your eudaimonic and hedonistic happiness cues.
- You have also sketched out your Happiness Life Plot and are starting to see where and how your happiness journey began.
- And you have explored and tried on for size different philosophies regarding happiness.

Acceptance

Introduction

We have claimed the ground upon which we stand, and are starting to feel into our own space by becoming more aware. You've got more awareness and clarity about you, your life and your happiness. Once you have become more aware in any part of your life, you get to make a choice. You get to choose to move onto the next step in your happiness journey, or not. It is time to move on to accepting what is. We have cleared away the weeds, dug up the buried bits of our past, and allowed awareness to soak in. Now let's feel about inside to see if we are able to accept what is in our lives.

You can think of acceptance as acknowledging the truth of the matter. The act of acceptance is the bridge between first becoming aware of a situation, and forgiveness. Acceptance asks for honesty with the truth of your life so that you can move forward. And, like any bridge you can choose to cross it or to turn around and stay on the familiar side. Even with acceptance, it is your free will choice what to do next.

You can accept what is and what has happened throughout your life, or you can choose not to act on your new awareness. You can choose to keep clearing the path forward into forgiveness, or allow weeds to come back and choke out what you have cleared so far. That is totally a choice you have the opportunity to make. It is up to you.

Acceptance doesn't just work on situations and other people. Wholly accepting who you are is a life-changer. It is freeing, empowering, and feels like it takes a weight off your shoulders that you didn't even know you were carrying. Further, acceptance allows us to be honest about our happiness needs, so you can create more of it.

On the other hand, refusing the gift of acceptance will keep you stuck and in repetition. Like I said, it is your choice, but eventually, swallowed and ignored traumas will show themselves. If not dealt with these traumas can cause ill health at some point. This is also where addictive and distracting behaviors can kick in to muffle that which we are trying to hide, or evade. Acceptance is seeing the truth. Forgiveness is about healing those truths. Understanding is about stepping into your complete power and how that manifests as a personal happiness practice.

In this section on acceptance we will explore the truth of

who we are. You will uncover and accept some of the ways you hold yourself back from happiness. (Yep, you really do that to yourself - it is pretty common!)

We will talk about emotional power, emotional labor, mother labor, and how accepting these big ideas relate to your happiness. It is so easy to hand your power over to someone else. I will introduce the idea of caretaking roles in owning your own emotions, and how taking responsibility for your reactions is a good path to deepening your happiness.

We will also talk about big ticket items like triggers and blocks. These guys can be protective (in the same way that training wheels are) and can be just as limiting. We will kick the concepts around until you thoroughly recognize the difference, and how they show up in your life specifically.

We will also play around with personality quizzes. I happen to think these are fun, and yes, I am a nerd. In all seriousness, it can be hard to accept our amazing qualities - or parts that need tweaking. Receiving a slightly more objective personality writeup can provide a better view of yourself.

I'll also discuss the two important terms of congruence and dissonance. No surprise that they they relate to our happiness! We will go into how to turn these to our advantage, rather than pushing back against them.

Your Emotional Power

Part of being a happier person is in staying emotionally empowered. This means keeping the responsibility to be happy as your own. It also means not taking on someone else's emotional burden. Have you ever felt responsible for someone else's happiness? Feels draining, right? Or, maybe you've hung your happiness on another person? Never feels like your needs are met, correct?

What if you could release yourself from that emotional bondage? What if you could create and sustain your own happiness without having to rely on someone else? You have the power within you now to do both. What would it feel like to be free instead of constantly making someone else happy? Or not to wait for someone else to blunder into the action you were really hoping for days later? How amazing would it be to sort both of these drama moments out for yourself?!

That will be our focus in these next few pages.

There are a couple of commonly-used terms that I'd like to share with you that will help clarify how this emotional responsibility dance works. I've included working definitions and examples below. If you would like more information on these ideas, I have added several links in the reference section for you.

Emotional Power is about taking responsibility for how

you feel. Being in your emotional power means that you do not allow others to have control over your happiness. Being able to care for your own state of being is the key here. This leads to you take responsibility for your own happiness (or lack thereof.)

We're all guilty of this at some point, as we all have to learn this lesson. I've done it too. It is a part of becoming emotionally intelligent. I realized I was using my husband to establish how happy I was with myself. If I got a compliment, I felt great. If I didn't, then the only possible explanation was that I was ugly. This made me completely UNhappy. I was giving away my emotional power, my happiness. To my husband. Learning how to keep emotional power, even as children, is incredibly important for our (happiness) sake.

Emotional Labor refers to the work involved in your own emotional management or support. When you feel down, sad or upset, can you get back to being okay on your own, or do you rely on others to do it for you? This relying on others for constant emotional support is sometimes called caretaking. As competent adults, it is our responsibility to carry our own emotional labor for ourselves. This is part of being in our personal power. However, we are often asked to emotionally labor for other competent adults. If we take on the emotional labor of others, it becomes a drain on our energy, time, and resources. This actually depletes us and takes us further from our own happiness work. (I have seen many adults do this, it is an easily learned pattern. But now we can do better, feel better, and hold our own energy. How exciting is that?)

To carry on with the above example from emotional power, I needed to do my own work (my own emotional labor) to become happy inside my own skin. I needed to be happy and confident with myself, rather than relying on someone else (even a loved one) to set my value. By taking this 'job' back over from my husband, I reclaimed the emotional labor of becoming happy with my body Self.

My Thoughts on This:

I have noticed sometimes we are reluctant to take back our emotional power and to independently emotionally labor because we think it inspires intimacy and closeness between partners. However, that has not been my experience. Once you are able to become a complete, powerful, happy, whole person yourself - the love, intimacy, and passion increases by a magnitude! If this part interests you - keep your eyes out for my next set of books.

The Mother Role is the emotional labor associated with the mothering role, but not restricted to actually being a mother. The difference here is when we are asking, or being asked, to caretake someone that isn't within our legit responsibility sphere. There could be other relationships of responsibility but these are the legitimate needs for emotional caretaking that come to my mind: a parent or guardian for a minor, caring for a non-competent adult, and a therapist / counselor / mentor / sponsor for another. Asking someone to be in the mother role takes emotional labor to the next level and implies a more active, longer-term role with more responsibility.

I own a massage therapy and wellness practice. It is very common for my clients to want to pass off their personal and emotional power and put me in charge of their healing journey. They want to be mothered, succored, massaged, and reassured that no change needs to occur on their part. They are hoping that I will take care of everything for them. What doctor to see, what medicines to take, what exercises to do… Not only is this beyond scope of practice and ILLEGAL, change has to be a choice.

Watch Out Woo:

I have three horses that I board at an amazing facility about two hours round trip away. As you can imagine, the commute makes it challenging to visit them as often as I would like. Further, it seemed like the little buggers were magnets for health issues. My paternal grandfather always said, 'Horses are fragile animals always looking for inconvenient AND expensive ways to die!' But I didn't remember our horses growing up being this accident prone! I felt like I was carrying their health and needed to be physically with them at all times. (Keep in mind that they are being boarded at an exceptional facility.) Finally, life, my businesses, a hard family death, ridiculous arctic weather, and my own health all came crashing down. I felt like I couldn't carry three horses in my energetic arms as well, even though I wanted to. I communicated with each, and while assuring them of my love, care, and help, explained that they each needed to be responsible for their own health. I couldn't hold the mother role for them any longer. Each being needs to be responsible for their own journey. Help is a wonderful thing to offer, but you can't do it for any one else. You can't exercise for someone else, you can't interview for someone else, you can't say no to pie for someone else. We are each responsible for our own journey.

The craziest thing? After that conversation, my horses are some of the healthiest and least problem-prone ponies on the place. Apparently, I finally learned that lesson.

By not agreeing to undertake someone else's emotional labor, we free up so much space and energy for our own happiness. It is time to only worry about our own stuff. I can't stress how important and life-changing this is, and it all starts with accepting the emotional space that we operate from. AND, it empowers the other person!

Learning More About the Mother and Child Roles

There are many ways the Mother Role can creep in and affect your happiness. We are going to cover two of the big ones here.

1. We can adopt the child role, and put someone else in the mother role, as we are looking to not be responsible for our own emotional power and happiness.
2. We can accept the mother role when someone else puts themselves in the child role.

I'm thinking that just about each and every one of us have either expected someone else to make us happy and to be our emotional crutch. Or maybe you've been shoved into the mother role for somebody else (not counting legit mother-child relationships). Adopting the child role can feel easy. This is when you want to be happy, and are asking others to take responsibility for your happiness and 'apply the lime' to your garden (instead of their own). It usually crops up when we are looking for external validation or external emotional bolstering. This shows up when you are feeling down and want someone else to make you feel better. Or maybe you aren't sure how you are doing in a certain situation, and want someone to repeatedly and continuously tell you how great you are. This want for external validation can come from partners, coworkers, families, bosses, friends... even strangers!

One of my past therapists is a perfect example of an adult taking the child role to extremes. She continuously asked for validation and compliments in her daily interactions. She seemed unable to self-start on the smallest task and yet seemed fully functioning in other aspects of her life. After numerous conversations, trainings, suggested readings, and modality walk-throughs I had to let her go. She did not want to take responsibility in the job, she was resistant to holding her own personal power, and wanted everyone around her to be in the mother role. This does not lead to success, self empowerment, or expression of your highest happiness.

What happens in your life when you have expected others to make you happy?

_____

_____

_____

Now, it is all about intention. It's not like the balance of power between partners is always going to be 50/50. There are times in relationships when we feel that we are not capable of being self-sufficient. There are times when we know deep down we are capable, and are merely choosing not to carry our own emotional weight. You have to accept the truth of what is happening.

My Thoughts on This:

When I first came down with histoplasmosis and fibromyalgia, it knocked me for a total loop. Getting a shower was a struggle! I literally used everything I had to chew and breathe. There was nothing left of me to give to being self-sufficient and caretaking my own emotional power. I relied on my husband to look after everything - the bills, the house, us! And my emotional well being, my happiness, my need for romantic bolstering... it was an incredibly vulnerable time.

Does this resonate for you? Can you think of a recent example when you maybe asked someone to caretake your emotional responsibility for you because you did not feel capable of doing it yourself?

_____

_____

_____

Asking for help is fine when you literally can't do it. Asking for love or connection from someone in a way that benefits BOTH of you (let's spread fertilizer on both gardens) is great! Asking someone to forgo their emotional needs and neglect their happiness to ensure yours is not okay. It all comes down to intention and honesty about what you can or can't do.

My Thoughts on This:

At a different point in my marriage I was totally guilty of this! I had a running litany in my head of things that my poor husband was supposed to do to keep me happy. Gifts, flowers, cards, notes, chores. If he didn't perform the tasks on command, WITH FEELING, I would end up in a tailspin because that meant 'he didn't love me.' Holy cow. Poor guy! I was giving away all my superwoman power to create my own happiness and was expecting someone else to do it for me. Wow. It was such a big awareness in my life that I featured it in one of my webinar series, 'Quit Giving Your Happiness Away'

Part 1 - https://youtu.be/FTgqsTtaRsA
Part 2 - https://youtu.be/LGOIwNVAfbo
Part 3 - https://youtu.be/_p95UClNpy0)

There are many problems with asking someone else to be responsible for your happiness. If you give someone else responsibility for you happiness, they can decide when and how to deliver it. That is a ton of power to be giving away. Don't you want to decide for yourself how you want to feel? Additionally, no one is a perfect mind reader. How can someone else possibly keep track of the ever-changing list of things needed to make you happy? That would be almost impossible.

And finally, no one takes care of someone else's property

to the standards of the owner. This is a fact of life. Even if the other person has the best of intentions. I love my husband dearly, but when you hand him a weedwacker, it is every plant for itself. Including the clump of hollyhocks I finally grew from seed! So, you need to attend to your own emotional needs, including your happiness, because it is your job to know them best. It gives us empowerment, courage, and a feeling of control over our own lives.

My Thoughts on This:
Also, just to throw this truth bomb out there... Very few people are feeling 'ok' at the moment, right? Everybody has a few things to clean up in their own energetic and emotional house. We all have some healing to do! So, why would you ask someone that might be struggling to get his own shit sorted out, to fix yours? Just sayin. This one hit me like a ton of bricks. Truth.

Be honest with yourself about a recent example that you can think of where you gave up your emotional power to someone else, (or even put someone in the mother role) when you were capable of taking care of your own emotional labor?

_____

_____

_____

What was going on in your life at this time?

_____

_____

_____

Were there any emotions you were feeling that felt tough to deal with on your own?

_____

_____

_____

Can you see a pattern emerging here? What is it?

_____

_____

_____

The converse of assuming the child role is allowing yourself to be cast inappropriately in the mother role. This means you are allowing yourself to be responsible for someone else's emotional labor. You are either making yourself responsible, or are being called upon by another to make decisions, bolster their self esteem and/or feed their needs. As I said before, this one is extremely common for women.

Women have been responsible for this for eons. You can end up in the mother role for your adult kids, your husband, your boss, your friends, your neighbors, and anyone else that you bump up against. Doing someone else's emotional labor takes time, energy, and sends the subtle message that your emotional state doesn't matter. This can definitely impact your happiness.

The Solution to Emotional Laboring

So what do you do when you no longer want to be responsible for someone else's emotional labor? One of my best friends, a very talented dancer, business woman, and independent therapist in D.C., Asha Gray, LCMHP, has a great phrase that she uses. It is about choices. Rather than trying to make yourself responsible for another's actions, release other people and their decisions, to their own journey by saying, "that's his/her choice and not my responsibility!" Say it with gusto!

You see a friend spend an outrageous sum on a heritage rose from England, when you know she has more 'responsible' places to put the dough. Go ahead and release that need to be responsible for her choice with the phrase, "That's her choice, her journey, and not mine!" Boom. Done. No further comment or thought needed.

When this same friend tries to get you to validate her purchase by making her feel better about it? It is your choice, and your journey. You get to decide whether or not to listen and give that support. Or maybe she wants you to feel guilty about why she can't afford lunch out? You can't be responsible for someone else's choices. The emotional labor associated with making decisions stays with the person making the decisions. I'm going to say that last part again:

The emotional labor associated with making decisions stays with the person making that decision.

How does knowing the situation has nothing to do with you, make you feel?

_____

_____

_____

Where in your life could letting go of this mother role benefit you and help you to be happier?

_____

_____

_____

Take a moment to reflect on a situation in your life that needs you to release some responsibility. How would it feel to release some of that responsibility with a "that's her/his choice" phrase?

___

___

___

___

___

___

___

Accepting the fact that you ARE NOT responsible for another competent adult's journey is overwhelmingly powerful and freeing. I have conducted over 100 interviews with people from all over the world about happiness, and one of the most repeated obstacles I have found is that people give away their own emotional power, their ability to be happy, to someone or something else. What they don't realize is that happiness is an inside job!

My Thoughts on This:
Obviously I am not speaking to situations in which you are:
a parent or guardian for a minor,
caring for a non-competent adult,
a therapist or counselor for another,

or anywhere you have legit agreed to the role of mother.

However, even where you are a legitimately in the mother role, I bet there is still plenty of room to shift some of the emotional labor and responsibilities. It will take time, training, patience, and boundary setting… but it can be done. And don't let the thought of this extra short term work get in your way. You being happy rather than hagridden is a worthwhile goal. So what responsibilities and emotional labor (that you might have honestly agreed to) would you like to shift? And how can you do this?

_____

_____

_____

Releasing our responsibility for someone else, and their happiness, can be tough. It can feel especially tough when someone's decisions are perceived to impact us. Just remember that there are all kinds of assumptions, excuses, limiting beliefs, growth blocks, and conditions going on in the background of that situation. It can take time, thought, and techniques to separate out and distance yourself from someone else's circus and monkeys. For now, just remember the phrase, "That's his/her journey." Just keeping this in your sphere will shift many things.

Knowing Your Personality Whys

That is why I always encourage people to learn their personal *whys*. Knowing our antecedent actions allows us all to get through to the understanding level of change (and to happiness) more quickly, rather than being in a continuous state of confusion and reaction. It has been my experience that attempting to move through something sticky, without getting to the root cause, doesn't give you a base to operate from. Its like planting a rosebush in the same place over and over, only to have them die on you. (Did you know soil can get 'rose-sick'?) Is the solution to continue to plant English roses that cost two arms and a leg and hope for better results? Or would it be more prudent (and overall more efficient!) to dig in and figure out what is the root cause of the problem? One of the easiest and fast things we can do to learn more about ourselves and our *Whys* is to take several personality quizzes or assessments. These quizzes can help us realize what is happening on a variety of levels and are fun! Some info will ring true and other bits will be far off to left field. Regardless of the level of accuracy, these answers allow you to get a feel for the space that you occupy.

A great personality quiz is known as the 16Personalities Quiz. It is based on the Myers-Briggs test. Find the link in the references (on page XX). I encourage you to check it out.

Record your results.

___

___

___

What really pops out at you and seems to resonate from the results?

___

___

___

What results did you receive that sound as if the Universe is speaking straight to you?

___

___

___

What is challenging in what you found out?

___

___

___

I also do a full personality profile if you would like a deeper understanding of yourself, and would like more personal help. That info is also in the back, on page XX.

My Thoughts on This:
For someone that was really upset about any labels being applied to me through my life, it is surprising that I am now eager and proud to apply them to myself.

I have discovered that I am an empath and an introvert. Learning these two things about myself has made a vast amount of difference to my happiness practice. Knowing who I am and how the world affects me has been a life-changer. I schedule in hermit time, I create boundaries around my space, and I am so much more accepting of my needs.

Emotional Triggers and Blocks

We've read the results of our personality test. You have decided what you are going to accept. You may know new things about your personality that you are working on accepting. But, your personality isn't the full definition of who you are. Another big part of who you are is how you react to your world. The next step is accepting your reactions. I introduce to you the idea of Emotional Triggers and Blocks.

Blocks are different than triggers in that they are more about action or emotional avoidance, denial, or mitigating our proper responses. Our subconscious is setting us up to experience less rather than falling into the deep pit of an emotional trigger. **Emotional Triggers** are when you experience increased emotion in reaction to something happening. When you get triggered, you usually experience more emotion and energy. Blocks and triggers can live in several places inside us. Further, since both can have multiple layers, it might take more than one time working with it to release it fully.

My Thoughts on This:
Emotional triggers and blocks are also similar in that they can feel like a loose thread. One little piece of string that is irritating, so we yank on it (one quick pull, right?) and end up unraveling the whole waistband of our underpants. Do you ever notice that the next time we find a loose thread we leave it alone? That's because we remember the big mess we made last time and don't want an emotional tangle to deal with so we ignore it. How we react to triggers and blocks is pretty much exactly like that!

One of My Triggers

One of the hardest areas for me to accept about myself has been around body image, my body-self. I have never been happy with my physical appearance. Not ever. Even looking back at older photos when I was pretty cute, I only saw the flaws. I remember wanting to shrink away from my skin, to hide, and even toyed with the idea of being a cutter as a teenager.

So it was a special kind of torture when I became a bodyworker, and gorgeous coeds would lounge around on my table. Perfect tan, perfect bleached teeth, perfect hair extensions, long fake nails, long fake eyelashes, tiny little bodies, and teeny little thongs. I was absolutely triggered by them showing up on my table. And I felt forced to do the bodywork.

I think it was the thongs that really got me to be honest. I have never found them comfy, and prefer full and complete coverage on my bottom, thank you. But I had internalized that and thought if I were thinner and perfect, then I would wear itsy bitsy thongs and like it. It was somehow a measure of my unattractive self that I didn't wear sexy undies. Know what I mean?

So I would literally grit my teeth, breathe deep, and try to be of service - all while loathing myself and mentally saying over and over again, "Eat some damn cake. Eat the cake, Eat the whole cake. Yummy yummy, have some cake!"

What can I say? It was totally an unhealthy coping mechanism. I know this. I am aware of it. And I accept that I was in survival mode, rather than my highest self.

But something amazing happened over this journey of happiness and discovery. I had been working on the love, acceptance, and forgiveness of myself (especially my body), but I hadn't really noticed the strides I was taking. I noticed I was more 'ok' with wearing a swimsuit in public, but that was about it for the physical side.

One day, a coed made it onto my massage table and I felt my hackles go up. I experienced the initial shrinking and pressure in my heart space. I thought, 'Uh-oh, here comes the cake!'

Then, that pressure inside left! This child, and her thong had nothing to do with me. Her journey and mine were in completely different directions. Her being no longer triggered me because I could accept, forgive, and love myself. Namaste. And isn't that bloody brilliant!? Being happy with yourself is the ultimate achievement.

My Thoughts on This:
When you can stay present, accept, forgive, and direct a previously triggering situation out of your sphere, give yourself a HUGE pat on the back! You have cleared that layer of that trigger. Congratulations! That is a major win for your happiness practice.

Your Self Centers

So let's lay out your beliefs in light of each of the self-centers (mind, body, spirit, emotions) to keep creating your happiness story. We are specifically answering for each of our self-centers because our modern life encourages us to fracture ourselves apart (another example of Cartesian Reduction). Because we label 'good parts' or feel we need to punish ourselves with the parts we hate and label them as the 'bad parts.' Being happy means accepting, forgiving, and loving our complete self, our creative artist, all of what makes us up.

On what path is your spirit? Do you have a spiritual practice?

_____

_____

_____

How do you practice or partake of your spirituality?

_____

_____

_____

Are you happy with where you are with your spirituality at this point in your life?

_____

_____

_____

What showed up in the personality tests for spirit?

_____

_____

_____

How do you experience your body?

_____

_____

_____

How do you feel claiming your body as yours?

_____

_____

_____

Are you happy with your body? What showed up in the Personality tests in regards to your physical body?

_____

_____

_____

What do you think about the state of your mind?

_____

_____

_____

Are you confident with your mental ability in life? At work?

_____

_____

_____

Are you happy with your thoughts? Are they uplifting, positive, and engaged?

_____

_____

_____

How do the results of your personality test match up against your mental day to day journey? Can something be tweaked to bring you more into alignment?

_____

_____

_____

What do you feel is your general emotional state?

_____

_____

_____

How does this match with your personality test?

_____

_____

_____

Is there anything here you would like to change? Ideas on how to make that happen?

_____

_____

_____

Action Steps for Change

This exercise is here to give you your action steps for becoming happier with each of your self-centers! Now for each mind, body, spirit and emotions, give at least one thing in the positive column (to recognize and appreciate your strengths) and one could-use-some-work item (we'll call these your action steps). Yes stick through this… don't skip this one. It will be easy to be hyper-critical here - we humans have that tendency. Try not to do that. Hell, you might even enjoy it!

These are your Action Steps for Change.

	Positive Column	Could Use Some Work
Mind		
Body		
Spirit		
Emotions		

Knowing your Action Steps for Change is big time. This not only gives you next steps for improving your happiness with each of your self-centers, the exercise also moved you through heavy self-acceptance, while allowing for improvement. Acceptance and change. These are two sides of a coin when it comes to having a happiness practice. Or another way to look at it is balance.

Think of it as watering… too much water will kill your plants by suffocating their roots. Too little water will dry them out and kill your plants. You need to balance the two sides to hydration.

Playing With Blocks

The other point of the Next Action Steps for Change exercise is to acquaint you with blocks, and how they affect your overall happiness. Why are blocks a problem? They can 'block' our growth, and stop us from planting better things! They get in our way. We can literally stumble over them. I don't believe you can be happy when you spend energy avoiding something.

So, did you want to avoid the Next Action Steps for Change section? Or were you reluctant to start? If the answer is no, sub in a recent time when you didn't want to do something you knew you needed to.

Did any of the five low emotions (sad, scared, angry, anxious, or depressed) crop up when you were working on that exercise? _____

Which ones?_____

If so, congratulations!! Chances are you found a block!
Often, when taking a look inside, you experience reluc-

tance, avoidance or vague anxiety. And this serves to block you from moving forward. Are you experiencing any reluctance, avoidance or vague anxiety in your life now?

Which one?_____

Humans Use Blocks For Protection

Under that feeling of reluctance, avoidance or vague anxiety, there is usually one, or more, of the five lower emotions: sad, scared, angry, anxious, or depressed. These five energetically low emotions function as a kind of protective lid over deeper, more vulnerable stories. When you are feeling one of these it can be a sign that you have found something big that limits your overall happiness.

Can you feel underneath your reluctance, avoidance, or anxiety and identify one of the five lower emotions that may be affecting you? Which one? Is there more than one?

_____

_____

_____

Currently it is thought that the hindbrain is the originator of blocks. The hindbrain detests swift change and prefers the ease of inertia. Change is exciting, scary, and energy expensive. Your brain can actually create physical sensations of dread, fear, and anxiety around change. It does this in an attempt to keep us safe. Historically, the first person that tried something new, usually died! They got eaten, drowned, poisoned, trampled… you get the idea. So our whole neural wiring is designed to keep us safe, and not to allow change. Even when change is necessary to be happier! Isn't that crazy?

I initially experience blocks as vague anxiety, or reluctance toward some action. When I strive to feel into what's going on below that, I usually get anger and depression. That is my **Low Emotion Cocktail** and it is a big hint that I have another hidden room to clear out. (See the acceptance of my own emotions there?)

In our rational world, talking about a vague anxiety or reluctance to taking an action isn't necessarily normal so we look for answers to explain the block. We come up with false rationalizations that keep us stuck in unhappiness. I wasn't very well going to tell my book coach that I hadn't completed a section because I felt too stupid or too fat to get visible! OMG. How embarrassing. How vulnerable! So, like most normal humans, I came up with logical and palatable excuses instead, or used avoidance strategies like being serially distracted, or too busy, or overwhelmed.

The trick to moving past your block is to feel into and below those more surface emotions. Under that resistance is where the lies and fibs we tell ourselves hideout. These lies and fibs are what we use to rationalize our fear. It is a phrase (maybe 2 or 3 phrases!) that pops into our mind that is usually short, kind of clichéd, and may sound kind of mean. In short, it sounds like a playground taunt. Some of the gems that I have uncovered for myself throughout my life are:

"You're too fat, too stupid, too ugly to be happy."

"No one will ever listen to what you have to say."

"You should quit, you'll never figure this out."

My Thoughts on This:
Yep, those are mine above. See, even though I KNOW this stuff, it can still sneak up and get me if I am not being aware.

What Low Emotion Cocktail do you see when you look under your vague anxiety or reluctance??

_____

_____

_____

What are the harsh lies that you've come up with that keep you stuck, or change-adverse? Look for words like: always, never, no one, everyone.

_____

_____

_____

Banishing Our Blocks

Do you see how a block that is at first perceived to be an emotion can make us shy away from change, or our true happiness, without really being aware of it? If we allow ourselves to accept those first reactions as truth, without further exploration, we stay stuck, unchanged, and frustrated. By going deeper, we find a level of protective responses that are our Low Emotion Cocktail. Buried under those lower emotions are the lies framed as short, usually mean phrases. These are the actual blocks. We come up with rationalizations for these blocks that are easier to share. All of this energy being spent is to prevent the feeling of vulnerability. That is the power of what blocks can do in our lives. Know also, that for most people, a good deal of this is done unconsciously. It is time to bring these blocks into the light of happiness where they can be accepted and released.

I visualize blocks as a hidden room, with a big KEEP OUT sign on the closed door. The initial vague reluctance/anxiety/avoidance is represented by the KEEP OUT sign itself. I could decide to not examine this space further. That is my choice. But I know that whatever is behind that door won't go away by ignoring it. With a bit of self-query or by using my Why Game (in the Understanding section), I can find my Low Emotion Cocktail around the issue represented by this particular door. Having lower emotions around something is a big hint that we need to open the door and determine what is really going on. When I open the door, the room beyond can look dark and scary. I would rather pull out a fingernail than admit that I'm scared of the dark and unknown, so I use my brain to rationalize a way out of dealing with myself. I come up with other excuses to not clean out the room - like, I am too busy, or it's such a small room that I can always do it later, or I have other things to do...

But no! This is where we can persevere by not accepting excuses the logical brain presents. This is the time I step further into the room. It can feel scary to do this. What might I actually find in this space? That I am ugly, dumb, fat, stupid, unloved, unworthy, not capable, unmarriageable, useless, an imposter? Whatever is REALLY your block on any particular issue?

Know that the only way to banish the monsters, is by

turning on the light. The light of truth. Our monsters, the daggers we carry in our heart, can't withstand illuminating truth. So I bring truth into the room and answer each lie to release it.

My Thoughts on This:

And a disclaimer. I am not saying ignore the feelings of fear and anxiety in every circumstance. Quite the contrary, fears or vague premonitions can save your bacon in many circumstances. Learning how to accurately interpret when you are actually in danger, and when your hindbrain is manipulating you is a big key to life and creating happiness!

To see the process of Banishing your Blocks from start to finish, let's go through the door again, together, and fill in the blanks.

What is the vague feeling you experience initially that is trying to persuade you that no change is need?

_____

_____

_____

Now, take a moment to visualize this block as a room, with a door.

What does the door look like to your room? Is there a sign on it? What does the sign say?

Watch Out Woo

You can even ask for help from Spirit to get a better grasp on this. Picture the door in your mind. Fill in the senses: smell, sight, sound, touch, taste. Feel your heartbeat. Touch your emotions. You are in front of this door... what are you feeling and sensing about what is behind it?

Where are you?

What else can you pick up that will help you place where your imagination (and Spirit) have placed you?

_____

_____

_____

That emotion, lessened to real world levels, is how your brain is trying to warn you away.

Ok, but you know there is something underneath of that feeling. That is your Low Emotion Cocktail. It is your sign to go deeper. What lower emotions are coming up for you?

_____

_____

_____

Once you have opened the door and have seen how dark and spidery it is, you are tempted to start rationalizing about why you don't need to go in. What are your most common excuses?

_____

_____

_____

But you are going to be brave and carry on lion-hearted! You step into the room and are beset with the gnashing teeth of the gremlins we carry around in our own heart and soul. See clearly, and name whatever is here. Name the lies that are your blocks to happiness, growth, change, possibilities....

_____

_____

_____

Finally, shed the light of truth in your room to finish the Banish the Block exercise.

With each lie, what is the actual truth? (Phrase it as a rebuttal and talk about why it is the truth). Please, please, please do this final step. It is an important part of the exercise.

_____

_____

_____

Knowing this Banishing Your Blocks technique is like knowing a secret to life. It is is like having pixie dust to sprinkle on situations that just aren't working for you. With a bit of effort, and introspection, you will be able to become aware of, and accept what is keeping you stuck and blocked. Amazing!

Now that you are familiar with uncovering the layers that keep us blocked, let's specifically look at blocks around your happiness. It is amazing how specific our psyches can work. One of my false rationalizations around happiness when I was younger was, "I will be happy when ____ happens." It was logical, made sense, and I hadn't delved any deeper. I certainly wasn't happy in the moment, so I had to rationalize that I would be one day. This was me accepting that attaching my happiness to something outside of myself, and putting conditions on it was an ok thing to do.

At different times in my life, I have found new lies around happiness. Like, I didn't deserve to be happy. That happiness didn't exist. Or that happiness doesn't last. Some of my clients have found the exact same lies and I wonder at this. Is it coincidence or convergence?

Then the rationalizations… because you don't want to be *that* person and look for a more palatable way to relate what you are saying. Like, I will be happy when 'x' happens, when I can take a break, I'm just really tired right now, etc. Sometimes we are just tired. Sometimes it is a rationalization that our brain kicks up to not go deeper. Insidious the way the layers of false protection can build isn't it? I find it so interesting how the mind will feed us one fib that is more acceptable to keep us from finding a more vulnerable one buried down a level.

What do you think your blocks are around happiness?

_____

_____

_____

When you hear the idea of being happy, what comes up for you?

_____

_____

_____

These deeper lies, although they feel sharp and cutting… have a 'nah nah nah nah boo boo' quality to them… I can totally revisualize those deep-seated blocks as a pack of kids on the playground because the lies are short, repeated, and cliched. What are the playground taunts you hear in your mind when you think of of doing something that makes you happy?

_____

_____

_____

Now, that was a life-altering bit of emotional work you just completed. The more experience you get working with blocks, the quicker you will be able to spot them. Pretty soon, you will be able to catch yourself in the act of letting a block dictate your actions and you will be able to move past it, right then! That's the ultimate in feeling accomplished and should be celebrated!

Matching Our Insides & Our Outsides

You and I have talked a whole bunch about blocks to your happiness, seeing the truth, and accepting what is. Let's jump tracks now and talk about another really important piece of acceptance: understanding and matching our emotions with our physical expression. I think about it in terms of bringing the plants and seeds to the soil. Sometimes what you've planned, isn't actually what happens. And sometimes, even with the best of intentions, our inside and outsides get out of step.

In terms of your happiness, the work we've done thus far is internal. Inside is where the base of your happiness actually begins, which is why we started there. It is now time for you and I to expand your happiness acceptance to include the external. Lets work with your body center here as well.

First, I want to address the idea of **Dissonance**. This word actually derives from musical theory. It means: a tension or clash resulting from the combination of two disharmonious or unsuitable elements (thanks Wikipedia). Basically, that's what we are talking about here. When things become disharmonious in your life.

You need to know how these ideas affect your happiness. There are two main kinds of dissonance: Cognitive Dissonance and Emotional Dissonance. Then I propose a third, that I am calling Energetic Dissonance. Basically, these terms describe being at odds with yourself in some way.

Cognitive Dissonance means you have *conflicting thoughts and perceptions* around something in your life. An example would be taking and drinking water from a plastic bottle, your thirst is at odds with what you know to be the environmental cost.

Emotional Dissonance is when you have *conflicting emotions* inside of your self in regards to a particular person or situation. One of the most common situations in which we experience emotional dissonance is by lending an ear to a friend when we really aren't 'feeling it' or don't feel like we have the emotional bandwidth to do so.

Energetic Dissonance is when you are not displaying or responding to a situation with the energy you are currently holding, for whatever reason. An example of energetic dissonance would be pretending to be less tired, more energized, bubbly, and exuding more energy than you really possess on a date.

Congruence, on the other hand, is when things are running harmoniously. Congruence is certainly a sign that you are setting yourself up for happiness! It shows that your insides and your outsides match.

By learning about dissonance and congruence, we are bringing together our insides and outsides. When we are living inauthentically, or in dissonance we feel out of balance, confused, maybe a little depressed or crazy. This emotional swirl makes being happy much much harder. When we consciously live into our happiness, we are in congruence.

My Thoughts on This:
The Holidays are ripe with examples of all types of dissonance! I'll show you the three I'm talking about above from my very own holiday adventures. I know and believe my family to be good people at heart, but I am having difficulty resolving their recent political choices (cognitive dissonance). I love them dearly and miss them, but would rather not go for the family Christmas. However, I will most likely end up going, and I will be hiding my own emotional turmoil while trying to enjoy what I can. Thus displaying emotional dissonance. As an introvert, I am sapped of energy after being with large groups of people, yet 'resting' comes with explanations that I don't always have the ability to deliver. So I interact with more energy than I really hold (energetic dissonance).

It is incredibly difficult to be happy when you are experiencing any type of dissonance. The body, mind, spirit and emotions long to be congruent and authentic and in balance. Just like happiness is a balance point, getting in a congruent space is a balance point of agreement.

My Thoughts on This:

An interesting question was brought up in one of my How to Be Happier Workshops. Why is it that we take on the manic or low energy of those around us? I personally believe congruence plays a part here. Our hindbrain recognizes that being different is dangerous, so it works to match us to our environment and helps us blend with the herd. Our emotional balance then becomes the job of our higher brain to logically work through what just happened.

If you are trying to act against your nature, or display emotions that are not congruent with what you are really feeling, it will guaran-damn-tee that you will have a hard time being happy. Realize that when you are in dissonance, your emotions are being bottled up. At times societal pressure requires we not become emotional, or that we stow it until we are somewhere private. It's not really acceptable to lose your shit, cry or get angry at the office. If you have to throttle down your emotions and display an inauthentic exterior, please get your external and internal spheres back into congruency as soon as possible. Remaining at odds with yourself does lead to trauma, ill health, stagnation, and desperate unhappiness.

To be clear, I am NOT suggesting that you immediately sync up your insides and outsides and get rid of the hard-won filter you have placed on your tongue. I am suggesting that you keep tabs on what emotions and intensity you have bottled up and find your own way to release those safely and in a healthy manner.

Can you think of any place in your life that you are acting incongruently through emotional dissonance? This is a place in your life where have you felt contrasting emotions around a person or situation? A place where you feel one way, but for whatever reason, you are not able to release, or discuss that emotion? How has that affected you, and/or the situation?

_____

_____

_____

What about cognitive dissonance? Where in your life have you held two contrasting thoughts about a person or situation? How has that affected you, and/or the situation?

_____

_____

_____

Lastly, what about energetic dissonance? Where in your life have you not been able to respond authentically to a situation because your energy on the inside didn't match what was happening around you?

_____

_____

_____

How did that dissonance feel and did it have any lasting effects?

_____

_____

_____

Can you see how staying in dissonance is NOT accepting your own truths?

_____

_____

_____

What do you think would happen if you stayed incongruent for a long time?

_____

_____

_____

Do you know anyone that has been incongruent for a long time? _____

Can you see it in behavior, mood, or actions?

_____

How would you sum up that person's life experience? Remember, you're not judging, but you are trying to learn and figure this out to move forward, so what do you perceive?

_____

_____

_____

Could dissonance block your own happiness journey? How?

_____

_____

_____

In today's world adults are often faced with situations that call for uncoupling our outward facial expressions, posture, and tone of voice from our insides and the actual thoughts and emotions we are having at that time. Young children are extremely authentic. However, that is not where we find ourselves as adults. As much as I might want to throw myself on the floor of the freezer aisle in complete frustration when my favorite ice cream isn't available, it is generally not considered an emotionally mature act. Being that congruent between my outward expression and internal frustration might be great for emotional clearing, but is probably ill-advised at the grocery store.

Bridging the Gap

You can bridge that gap created when you are in dissonance by doing a high energy activity. I was just gifted the opportunity to experience this myself. I was at the accountant's office and received some potentially bad news. I became distraught and upset, and filled with panic energy on the inside. But, I certainly didn't want the accountant to know that. Plus, all of that emotion and fear gets in the way of seeing possibility and logical thinking. I excused myself from the meeting for a moment and went outside. On the sidewalk I did a quick set of lunges, jumping jacks, and knee-highs. This frenetic physical activity allowed my built up anxiety-energy to smooth out and allowed me to get energetically congruent very quickly. In less than 5 minutes I was able to calmly rejoin the meeting and logically work toward a solution.

Being emotionally, cognitively and/or energetically dissonant at the same time makes it incredibly hard to function, let alone be happy or present. It certainly doesn't allow you see possibility. It also usually means you are being triggered! I had to leave the room to deal with my situation, and calm back down.

Like I said, you won't always be able to get congruent in all places all the time. So try it yourself… If you can't get into emotional congruence, try to match your energy levels. This helps you feel more congruent and less cray cray!

In any of the examples of dissonance you gave above, is there a small step or action you could take to help you be a little more authentic? (I am not always able to react in the moment the way I would wish. So for me, I find it best to plot out scenarios and responses ahead of time. Maybe this could help you too?)

_____

_____

_____

Or do you want/need to remain dissonant for the moment? Why?

_____

_____

_____

My Thoughts on This:
I have found even just taking a moment to think it through is helpful. When you get strategic and think the situation through, stowing emotions can become a choice, instead of getting reactionary. I could choose to have a complete screaming fit with my coworker… but it isn't going to help and will only make working relations harder.

Sigh.

Ok. I choose NOT to do that.

Differently, I choose not to get into a political debate on Christmas eve. I also choose my own sanity by giving myself permission to leave if anyone else brings up politics. Because I set some healthy boundaries up front in order to deal with all of the political discussions, I was able to be present and not reactionary, at my grandpa's last Christmas. Don Gunnell, aka Bop, passed January 14, 2018.

Many people can get stuck in their head. Its normal in our society. We're trained to be in our mental space. If you are having a hard time with this section and struggling to come up with examples of dissonance, and how to fix it... you are not alone. It is fairly common for us to be out of touch with our insides, and how we automatically tamp down our reactions to what is considered polite and comfortable. Sometimes we even say, "I don't know what to think," as a very telling slip of the tongue when asked how we feel about something.

Has that ever happened to you? Substituting our logical mind instead of using our emotional self? When?

_____

_____

_____

If you think you need more help with getting congruent, you might want to try equine facilitated work. Equine coaching is particularly effective for showing humans how to plug back into their authenticity and congruency. The horse is much more emotionally and energetically reactive than a human. Horses have an innate distrust of emotional or cognitive incongruence as this can indicate sickness or danger in the wild. Horse is a great teacher in showing people how to heal the divide between our mind, body, emotion and spirit selves.

Is there anything you would like to incorporate into your own life and responses from this group? How do they inspire you?

_____

_____

_____

My Thoughts on This:
I have been an Equine Guided Educator and equine experience facilitator for over five years now. An equine coaching session is a graceful and transcendent way to make your internal energy and emotions visible through the horse's body. Horses are incredibly sensitive to intention, follow-thru, and energy levels and can translate that into very real terms for us humans. A healthy horse is usually and naturally congruent. They are a perfect bio feedback system for lost people.

Now, let's bring it all together. Let's compare - without judgement - how our old approach to happiness can be upgraded with this new intel. By bringing in your discoveries and acceptance of your emotional responsibility, personality type, life plots, and where we have been incongruent as an adult, we are seeing how our garden blueprint (your old idea of happiness) doesn't actually fit your real world, real life garden. Accepting who we actually ARE will enable us to craft a more authentic, happier life:)

My Thoughts on This:
I talk a lot about choice in this handbook and my workshops, and yet it is one of the harder concepts for people to grasp. It is hard to visualize 'choice' as it isn't tangible and the results might not be tangible either. One of the ways I have found to illustrate the idea of choice is to MAKE it about a real object with clear options. For instance, I can't plant tea bushes outside in Illinois and expect them to live. The choices are: 1) I might be able to house one indoors with a lot of expense. 2) I could move to where I can grow them. Or, 3) I content myself with growing mint, lavender, and lemon verbena for an herb tea. See how simple the concept becomes? It is the exact same thing with growing your happiness. You have to accept WHO you are and WHAT you need so that you can make informed decisions about what is possible, what you can compromise on, or what is an absolute for you.

Summing Up Acceptance

Yay!!! Another section completed!! This section was about strengthening our ability to see our ourselves and accepting what we find as it pertains to our happiness journey. By knowing ourselves more clearly, we can consciously create a life experience that both supports our needs and increases our happiness.

In this section we have learned about:

1. Emotional power, emotional labor, and mother labor. We learned the differences between each one, and how these ideas relate to our happiness.
2. You have seen some real-life examples of what it looks like when and how we give our emotional power to others, and how that causes problems in your life.
3. We have experimented with 'releasing another person's emotional burden using the phrase, "That is their choice. Their choice and outcome are not my responsibility." You remembered that you are not responsible for decisions made by other competent adults.
4. You played with personality quizzes to could get a better awareness, and acceptance of who you are, and how you interact with life. We also considered these quiz results in light of our four self-centers (mind-body-emotions-spirit) and what that can mean for your happiness
5. I talked about triggers, and how they affect your happiness.
6. I brought up the hind brain's role in keeping you safe from change. I also discussed how the hindbrain gives rise to blocks. These blocks keep us from taking the actions that would create more happiness.
7. We explored the Banishing Your Blocks exercise and discussed how to turn on the light of truth. We

grasped the idea that truth is the ultimate Block Buster and how it is a big part of acceptance.

8. I reviewed the concepts of dissonance and congruence, inside and out. I also talk about hy it is important to your happiness to make time to become congruent as soon as possible. We also explored the Match Insides & Outsides exercise and my own contribution to this arena, that of ENERGETIC congruency.

Forgiveness

Introduction

We are on fi-yah! So far, we have become aware of our happiness space and groped around internally to see what's there. We have faced our truth in acceptance. In this section on forgiveness, we will discuss giving back what no longer serves us so that we can fully experience happiness and balance in life. We'll do that through taking a look at the idea of forgiveness and what it really means. We are also going to look at old emotional patterns (that we may have picked up from others) and releasing those too.

In this section we will learn how forgiveness is one of the biggest gifts we can allow ourselves. We'll discuss how this simple idea is actually one of the biggest obstacles we face in being happier and healthier. We will talk about where and when we learn our emotional responses, how that impacts our happiness, and why forgiveness might be necessary in this area. I will be sharing a few amazing forgiveness techniques, including my Healing Forgiveness Statements and exercises that allow us to truly release and forgive from the heart - not just pay lip service to the idea.

A Little On The Word…

Knowing my love of word etymology, I had to sneak at least one into this book. The word *forgive* is pretty fascinating. Although the exact derivation is difficult, it appears to come from the Latin word *perdonare* and is defined as: to give completely without reservation. The Germans and French played with the word a bit, kicked it around, and tweaked the definition every decade or so. It popped back out in Old English as 'forgiefan' and meant: to relinquish a claim. So the truer meaning of the word *forgive* is meant to be: an all-encompassing release of debt, reserving nothing in this act of clemency. My goal is for you to forgive with open hands and heart, reserving nothing, and granting yourself clemency. It doesn't mean you are okay with the situation. It simply means you no longer carry this particular burden around with you every moment of the day.

My Thoughts on This:
Trust me, forgiveness clears the way for you to find peace and happiness. It is sooo good for you. I have never heard anyone rue the fact that s/he was able to forgive someone, and move on with life. Never. What does that say?

A Public Service Announcement on Forgiveness...

Forgiveness can get sticky. In order to truly forgive you need to look at situations in your life that you may have buried. If you have some bad memory files you'd rather not go into, that's okay. For our purposes in this handbook, you can set the intention of where you want to go and where you don't. Be clear and firm in your intention, and you can choose to not go into memories you don't wish to explore. You may also choose to seek professional counseling for some of the more traumatic spots. You do what you need to support yourself and your healing. Please know that whatever approach you take is brave.

I can't conceive of a more honest and gripping way to describe the importance of learning forgiveness than what Holocaust survivor, Eva Kor said,

"My forgiveness ... has nothing to do with the perpetrator, has nothing to do with any religion, it is my act of self-healing, self-liberation and self-empowerment. I had no power over my life up to the time that I discovered that I could forgive…when a victim chooses to forgive, they take the power back from their tormentors… but it is a choice."

You can learn more about Eva and read the full interview at this link: *http://www.npr.org/2015/05/24/409286734/its-for-you-to-know-that-you-forgive-says-holocaust-survivor* . Eva showed me how powerful forgiveness actually is. Her strength and honesty blow me away. I realized that forgiveness isn't found in small hearts, nor weak ones. Its found only in the brave (and yes, you can do it too). It is my intention to walk my path with the same authenticity and strength as Eva.

One of my own clients shared with me her incredibly brave freedom-through-forgiveness narrative. Notice what effect that forgiveness had on her body! I have paraphrased and consolidated it, but this is E's story:

"I have been trying various alternative methods and medication for chronic constipation over the last two years. I never told any of my counselors or therapists that I had been date-raped when I was 15. I thought I was over it. However, I finally got it that I hadn't forgiven him. That was what I was holding on to and couldn't let go of. That is what kept coming up in the sessions I had with you. But I kept thinking it couldn't be that. I was over it. Finally after almost

2wks with no bm, I was desperate to try anything! I felt like I was going to explode! I went into forgiveness and forgave him. I let go of hate and judging. I let go of the loathing and forgave myself. I forgave. For me. It had nothing to do with making his life easier. I was ready to let go for me. That night I cried a lot. The next day I had a bm. I have been regular since."

Like I said, for a long time I thought forgiving was a sign of weakness. I thought and felt in my soul that forgiveness meant the perpetrators got to skip off scot-free while I still had the work of trying to pick up the pieces, heal, forget, and limp on. Anger was my constant companion, and I thought that gave me power. Anger and rage burned inside. I thought those two hot flames would make me invincible. I am eternally grateful that I was given the opportunity to learn the truth without a bigger, more painful lesson.

I, and many others throughout history, have held the incorrect belief that anger and hate are protective. The truth is that anger and hate are not protective. Anger and hate are like drinking poison, and hoping the other person dies. They actually cause ill-health, and open the door to disease, bad karma, and stagnation of the soul.

Each of the great religions speaks of hate and anger because they are primal forces to be reckoned with. In the King James Bible, Proverbs 10:12, "Hatred stirreth up strifes: but love covereth all sins." And, 1 John 2:9-11, "He that saith he is in the light, and hateth his brother, is in darkness even until now. He that loveth his brother abideth in the light, and there is none occasion of stumbling in him. But he that hateth his brother is in darkness, and walketh in darkness, and knoweth not whither he goeth, because that darkness hath blinded his eyes." Just like in Proverbs, my experiences and those of my clients show again and again the same thing: anger feels protective and powerful, but in fact, it makes you weak and unable to see the greater truth. It also robs you of your happiness.

Forgiveness, on the other hand, is powerful and transformative. It does not mean forgiveness is easy or comes naturally for most of us. Mostly because we aren't taught how to really forgive when we are young. So we pick up this other habit instead.

Forgiving, and being free of past upsets and traumas does require a trade. It isn't free. The cost of your freedom is being vulnerable. You have to actually experience the grief or pain in order to let it go. That may not sound like a whole lot of fun, but, in return we receive lightness, happiness, and more joy. It is an incredible trade all-in-all, but it certainly isn't free.

The Maori are an indigenous Polynesian tribe native to New Zealand. They believe pain is trauma leaving the body. There are several schools of Structural Integration (another style of bodywork) that assumes this as well. They've been clear on this trade of feeling the pain in order to release it.

My Thoughts on This:

The act of purging possessions is very similar! Have you had the experience of finding it difficult to get rid of something you own? Sometimes things are hard to let go of, merely because we have owned them so long. This usually means that we are reluctant to experience change, and grieve during the release. Humans don't just collect tangible things. We hold onto emotional blocks, beliefs, and limitations too.

How do you feel about being able to forgive others? Does it feel easy?

_____

_____

_____

Is there any person or situation in which you find forgiveness especially difficult to muster?

_____

_____

_____

Why do you think it is hard for you to release this situation, and forgive?

_____

_____

_____

What do you feel about forgiveness as a gift for you, as opposed to the forgivee?

_____

_____

_____

If you could forgive, freely and easily, would that change things for you? How?

_____

_____

_____

My Thoughts on This:
Personally, I have also been learning that it is not just about forgiving what happened, but also forgiving what didn't happen. A few months ago one of my friends was making fun of his father's dad-jokes. It caught me because my brother and I didn't have that kind of

joking and affectionate relationship with our father. The communication wasn't there. I never received a card, letter, email, or text from my father. I had no voicemail to save. I literally don't have a way to understand the idea of a dad-joke. I've had to learn how to forgive that absence in my life. The lack of loving communication with my father has been one of the hardest things I have ever had to forgive.

Releasing as a Part of Forgiveness

I use garden metaphors so often because I feel that they are visceral symbols about life, change, and being resilient in the face of challenging circumstances. Because, what is more resilient than nature? Sometimes we have to change, rearrange, or even remove things that don't work - from our gardens - and from our lives. Forgiving of old resentments and patterns we picked up from others makes way for what is now, what is new, what is more expansive, and gives the best opportunities for happiness. (I.e. don't hang on to the invasive creeping ivy you planted on a whim… just because you thought you liked it 10yrs ago! Let it go, dig it up, and see what else is possible!)

Our emotional responses to situations are well-imprinted by the time we hit puberty. We learned the pattern of how to respond from watching and absorbing the actions and intentions of those around us. Emotional responses are the basis for how we interpret and interface with life. Here are some introspective questions to ask yourself about your own learned responses. Remember, we are not assigning blame here. We are not creating excuses for behaviors. We are becoming aware of patterns, accepting the truth of how they have operated in our lives, and forgiving these patterns in order to release them. This creates real freedom. Remember, the more forgiveness work you do, the more compassionate and happy you become!!

How do you deal with anger?

_____

_____

_____

Why is that your response?

_____

_____

_____

How do you experience disagreement?

___

___

___

What's a good way to share power in a relationship?

___

___

___

How do you interact with others?

___

___

___

Can you easily show love?

___

___

___

What about grief?

_____

_____

_____

How do you feel about being vulnerable?

_____

_____

_____

How do you show and accept love?

_____

_____

_____

You may be feeling emotional at this point. And a little vulnerable. That is totally normal. Stick with me. Keep reading. We'll process through it together. If it feels too intense, please reach out for support.

Emotional Reactions

Emotions, and how those around us expressed them, seep into us as children. Those responses if unchecked, flow back out of us as our adult emotional responses. Did you know that emotional responses can be traced back through generations? I have been able to track behavioral patterns in my own family up to five generations to my great-great grandparents. Think about it, one hundred forty-three years of passing down the belief that happiness is frivolous and a waste of time! This is why unearthing these patterns takes some conscious effort.

It is when I stumble onto these sorts of discoveries that I rely heavily on a quote from one of my favorite authors, Sylvia Jorrin. Paraphrased, "We all represent the difference between our parents being too good and not good enough." What is magical though is that people can change. It only takes one person, in this case me, to consciously change our family legacy for my brother's kids. I don't want to pass that belief on to someone else.

Those old emotional patterns of behavior might no longer serve you, or the situation you find yourself in. I used to 'wait for the other shoe to drop.' Just wait for the next thing to happen, staying a little keyed up and anxious, anticipating the next part of life to sideswipe me. It might have kept me safe when I was younger, but this emotional response was getting in my way as an adult. Being able to uncouple yourself from negative energy and negative emotional patterns is incredibly freeing and creates room for more happiness. Releasing those old patterns through forgiveness allows you to be happy and maintain your own energy even if those around you are invested in lower energy. Through forgiveness we can move into a space where we allow ourselves to plant what we want in our own garden. To grow it as we see fit!

I LOVE Anne Lamott. This is one of my favorite pieces of her writing, and it is on forgiveness.

> *I really believe that earth is forgiveness school – I really believe that's why they brought us here, and then left us without any owner's manual. I think we're here to learn forgiveness. For me, it begins with the hardest work of all, of being so crazily imperfect, and so sensitive and thin-skinned, and looking the way I look instead of like Cate Blanchett, which is disappointing. And all of the things we internalize in our younger years that other people might have said or hinted or even bullied us for. To forgive someone is the hardest work we do.*

I finally realized that the whole shoe dropping thing was actually a pattern around happiness! It was a, "Yeah, I might be happy now, but just wait till something happens. Happiness doesn't last." The pattern of not trusting happiness or ease or prosperity was deep and many generations old. However, I reached a point where that pattern no longer served me or provided for my needs. It was getting in my way of creating my business for myself. Of even writing this book! Because, why start things, or take any risks in life if they'll just end up blowing up in your face?

I became aware of the pattern, I accepted its role in my life (and my ancestors' lives), and I started the process of witnessing every time it showed up in my life - which was a lot. Every time I witnessed it, I forgave myself and my family for our human limitations. Now, when I'm about to make a move that shows I'm waiting for the other shoe to drop, I can make a happier, more empowered choice. That empowered choice looks like taking action - even when it's scary - to create what I want. HOW COOL IS THAT?!

In order to uncouple yourself from your old reactions and forgive for yourself, let's dig into what patterns you may have picked up in those formative years. How did the people around you express emotion? Which emotions were frequently present? Is there anything that stands out in your memory?

_____

_____

_____

How did these expressions of emotions make you feel? What do you remember thinking and feeling about it at the time?

_____

_____

_____

Do you see a similar response in yourself that you have picked up from the people close to you? If you can, give both an empowering, and a disempowering example.

_____

_____

_____

Is there a pattern here that you have absorbed that you would like to either embrace, or forgive and release?

_____

_____

_____

Do you think you are ready to forgive the responses you family has had in those triggering situations? Please also write in why you are ready.

_____

_____

_____

Instead of heaping anger and blame on yourself for picking up these learned responses or to the family from which you absorbed them, how would it feel to be able able to lovingly forgive yourself and them for that learned response?

_____

_____

_____

Can you remember a specific time you responded in this pattern? Take a moment to recall it now. Are you ready to forgive yourself for it? Without blaming anyone else? Why or why not?

_____

_____

_____

Your Healing Forgiveness Statement

Now… prepare for a big chunk o' healing to come your way! Direct from the Universe to you.

Rewrite that last stretch of questions and responses into a Healing Forgiveness Statement. Here is a quick sketch of how to do it:

1. From whom did you learn the pattern you'd like to release?
2. What did you internalize from that person?
3. What are you forgiving yourself and the other person for around this pattern?
4. Finish with: "This is no longer mine, I forgive and release this pattern."

My Healing Forgiveness Statement might look like:

I forgive my father for not seeking out emotional healing for himself. I forgive my father for teaching me his belief that being happy is selfish and pointless. I forgive myself for internalizing his approach to happiness. This is no longer mine, I forgive and release this limiting pattern around happiness.

Forgive & Release Exercise

Let's take that Healing Forgiveness Statement and release it. This is the practice I go through when I'm working to actually forgive and release. I hope you give it a try. When used repeatedly, it shifts the energy of your situation and creates healing for you.

Feel it: Feel the emotions it brings up, but remember you don't have to go back to that moment. Set the intention of what you are 'allowing' and hold those mental boundaries. (If this doesn't feel safe for you, this might be an exercise to explore with a therapist.)

Hold it: Hold the emotions of anger, strife, angst, fear, terror, rage, irritation… whatever they are surrounding the instance you are going to release. Take a big breath in. Bring your middle finger to your thumb like you are going to flick away a bug, and put a decent amount of tension in that finger position.

Let it GO! Simultaneously exhale loudly, flick your fingers, and picture yourself releasing this energetic, mental, emotional load as a grayish cloud. It is no longer part of you.

Follow Through: Envision this cloud floating away. It is no longer yours to carry. Or, you could blow it away from you, or picture a sparrow winging it upwards out of sight…

The important part is that you see it moving far away from you, off into the distance, and be truly gone from your sphere. I always include a prayer that the energy be transformed to good.

What is another Healing Forgiveness Statement that you would like to release?

1. From whom did you learn the pattern you'd like to release?
2. What did you internalize from that person?
3. What are you forgiving yourself for around this pattern?
4. Finish with: "This is no longer mine, I forgive and release this pattern."
5. Do the Forgive & Release Exercise

What was your biggest takeaway from this Healing Forgiveness Statement exercise?

_____

_____

_____

My Thoughts on This:
Healing Forgiveness Statements really do affect your world. When my husband and I got pets, I received INSTANT awareness on how I responded to emotion and happiness. Our new puppy was so sweet, but

also loud, boisterous, and constantly looking for stuff to get into. I was not emotionally experienced on how to handle that much energy all up in my grill. My instinct was to get mad and shut him down as a means of self-protection. And then it hit me... that I had a possible explanation for some of my parents' behavior. These same things happened to me when I was young, loud and boisterous. My parents (and their own lack of happiness or emotional awareness) could not handle it. I was watching myself do the same thing. It's not an excuse, but an explanation. Knowing that makes it easier for me to forgive myself, my family and write my Healing Forgiveness Statements. That's how powerful this forgiveness work can be!

Go back and look at your Healing Forgiveness Statements... are there any Mother or Child Roles at play? Which ones? Does that give you any more insight into the pattern you released?

_____

_____

_____

My Thoughts on This:

In my quest for holistic healing, I have been blessed to experience numerous Indigenous Healing Traditions and differing viewpoints regarding life truths. The Maori believe it is our bones that hold trauma, the bones are our secret-keepers and memory holders. If you can find a proper Maori Healer, Romi Romi work is an incredible, emo-

tionally clearing experience. The Maori work I have received was visceral and facilitated deep healing work. It helped me clear a lot of old traumas I'd been carrying around.

So we are going deep, to the bones. How did the pattern you released above affect you throughout your life? What effects did that pattern have in your life? We want to look at these things as well.

_____

_____

_____

Forgiving is something we do for ourselves. It is taking back our power, becoming stronger, becoming whole again - through the value of vulnerability. Every time you hold a grudge, or harbor a situation that has not been forgiven, you are giving away your emotional power. We've spent time here today taking your power back from situations and people to whom you've given that power. I hope you feel lighter, more loving, and more able to access your happiness each and every time you forgive.

The One Daily Ritual I Keep

This is actually one of the few things I remember to do for myself on a daily basis. Experts will tell you, "Just take seven minutes to be mindful." "Five minutes to hydrate." "Take fifteen minutes to focus on your breathing." "Always moisturize when you get out of the shower." On and on. If you actually did the complete supposed-to morning or evening practice list, you wouldn't have time for anything else! I am not going to say you should do this everyday, I am just going to share that my forgiveness practice is the only daily ritual that I keep. I am pretty flexible with the when, as long as it is after I've shut down for the night.

I take a cup of tea and my journal and close my eyes and think back through my day.

Was there anything that got to me?

Was there anything that made me feel bad?

Anything that I did that might have negatively impacted another?

I jot each down and weigh them.

Are there actions or restitutions I need to make?

I jot any of those down. And then work my forgiveness mojo on each situation using the practices I described above. I hope to reach a point where my forgiveness game is so on point that this occurs naturally and in the moment. But for right now, this is my one daily practice.

I can't begin to describe how my much this has changed my life. I feel freer, lighter, and happier. I can release grudges and I have noticed physical improvements to my health as well.

If you want to try it once and see how it feels, this is the formula I use, quick and simple.

	From Me	Toward Me	Releasing Statement
(Action/Situation)			
(Action/Situation)			

Summing Up Forgiveness

Holy Toledo, that was deep! I am so proud of you for continuing your journey into increasing your happiness. To do nothing is the easiest response and takes the least amount of effort. Any change takes energy and application. I am so proud of you for standing up and demanding more for yourself!

Forgiveness is about releasing that which doesn't serve us any longer. Forgiveness is ditching the weight, releasing trauma, and harbored grudges so that we can be lighter, freer, clearer, and make more time and space to be happy and healthy. In this section we have:

1. Learned how forgiveness is really a gift to ourselves and can be a major obstacle to allowing healing and happiness into our lives!
2. We explored the truth that anger and hate are not protective, and why forgiveness is the most powerful choice.
3. Experimented with forgiving people / circumstances using Healing Forgiveness Statements and took note of how that made us feel.
4. Discovered where we picked up how to emotionally respond.
5. Learned how to recognize our emotional responses as patterns.
6. Started the process of forgiving that patterning.
7. Introduced the connection between grief and vulnerability and happiness.
8. Talked about my one daily practice of forgiveness that I keep.

Understanding

Introduction

Each stage of *My Happiness Handbook* (awareness-acceptance-forgiveness-understanding) has an element of heavy lifting and self-actualization. This is both an exercise to do now, and something to continue to work on as a goal. What you've been doing is work, but there are many rewards along the way that are worth the sweat equity. Understanding is the time to enjoy your harvest.

Lets recap all of the amazing things you've done to work towards your happiness. We found things out about ourselves in the awareness phase that we didn't know or hadn't put together. No more delusion. Self awareness is like having the gift of clairvoyance, for your own life. To be able to see yourself clearly is a gift. Without that sight, it makes creating happiness so much more difficult. Ferreting out your actions and interactions with mindfulness is the first step to making happiness an irrefutable part of your life.

Acceptance grants the gift of receiving the truth and being able to grow through it with grace. Feeling strife, resistance or braciness about a part of your life? This is where acceptance is needed most. Consciously creating happiness is about moving forward in your journey.

And then we started working through forgiveness. This can feel like the most freeing of the stages. Although it can feel like a sisyphean task early-on, forgiveness gets easier and more fluid the more you do it. You will actually start to crave being free of resentments, anger, grudges, self-blame, and all the other little gremlins that like to ride around on our shoulders.

In this section we will talk about understanding and uncovering the gifts you were born with. I will share a few ways you can actually see and hear your gifts. I have found that a major component of being happy is to have a clear sense of the self, and how we relate to our external world. By understanding your own empowerment, you can be more confident, happier, and have a better shot at living in balance and harmony.

I have also included, as promised, a few of my favorite exercises to create more possibilities and to clear the blocks to happiness that are right in front of your feet. We will also reach the lotus of *My Happiness Handbook* by deliberately crafting your own happiness practice. This understanding section is where we bring the techniques and exercises together and allow something stupendous and unique to bloom for each person.

Some of the wisdom I have shared in this book is from masters of other fields and other indigenous cultures. I am utterly fascinated with ancient and traditional healing practices. Science (like ethnobotany, physics, chemistry, neurology, psychology...) now prove the power and efficacy of these original, native schools of wisdom. As explained in *Dawn Again, Tracking the Wisdom of the Wild* by Doniga Markegard, "The neuroplasticity research stating that it's on the cusp of a revolution, is essentially putting scientific terms to the beliefs of native hunter-gatherers. It's more like we are on the cusp of a ten-thousand-year-old science." It is understanding and relearning these holistic skills, that are both ancient traditions, and recent scientific discoveries, that gives me hope in humankind's ability to achieve greater balance in the future.

I get excited about combining traditional wisdom and science. In fact, my work has long been centered at the crossroads between science and woo. The information found at this intersection is ripe with magic and transformation… What could be more exciting than to deliberately explore what our ancestors knew and apply that to our own health and wellness today? I think people need to have a clear grasp of how recombining what we used to know with what is modern, is itself something new, exciting, and worthy of deep discovery.

A gardening example would be the lavender rose. Roses have been revered for about 5000 years and were first bred in China as pink, white, or red specimens. Other hues on the color wheel were eventually bred in. However, blue or lavender remained elusive until 1957. Gladys Fisher caused a stir in the horticultural world by breeding the first lavender hybrid tea rose and christening it Sterling Silver. It was the closest color to blue that had ever been seen in roses, with stronger fragrance, darker leaves, and was thornless to boot. Sure, there are roses, and yes, that pale lavender color is present in other flowers (lilacs for example), but by combining several traits in separate flowers into one, the floral world had something new.

Transcending Your Past

Let's talk about taking your forgiveness work to a whole new level of understanding. We are working to forgive, and yet it is really easy to stay stuck in the energy of the situation. How much more powerful could you be if you weren't carrying this around? Your past, no matter how nasty, can be a powerful force for change in your future. Transcending is not about surviving your past. It is about thriving, and helping others to live a better life as well. This is my definition of happiness. This handbook has been a journey, walking us through a learning and healing process so that we can consciously create our own happiness. In my experience, it is hard to go forward until you know where you came from, and what part of your history is impacting your present actions.

While our past can shape our present, it doesn't have to negatively impact our future. Does that seem easy, or difficult to believe? Why?

_____

_____

_____

If you are having a hard time envisioning a happy future, lets get a better understanding of what is in the way. Why wouldn't your future be happy?

_____

_____

_____

What would you say if you were given the opportunity to release those fears of the future?

_____

_____

_____

Usually, it is your own inability (my grandmother calls it lack of imagination) to mentally and emotionally picture different outcomes for yourself that is the trigger to staying stuck. If we can easily spend hours and energy anticipating depressing, scary and horrible times, why not spend those same hours and energy visualizing happy, joyful, meaningful times instead? What you focus on grows. In my pessimistic phases of life, I disdained the idea that I could think up new outcomes for myself because it was a daydream. I didn't think it mattered.

Not only was thinking that way an extremely limiting way to approach life, it also hampered my ability to be happy. In fact, I was miserable, cranky, rude, and angry! Not realizing your true potential, not believing in your own power, not having a sense of the possibilities swirling around you leaves you with a life half-lived.

I had no faith and no personal experiences to bolster a belief that there was more to the world than what our physical senses told us about. What I didn't know at the time was that I only had to look around to see the possibilities and real life magic. For example, one of the most infamous is the study conducted by Dr. Masaru Emoto in Japan that captured the difference in the structure of frozen water molecules by exposing them to different intentions.

Dr. Emoto used double-distilled water bought from the same company, exposed each non-control batch to a set of thoughts or intentions, flash froze the samples, and photographed the crystalline structures. Some of these samples were set as controls and received no intentions, prayers, or negative thoughts. Another set of samples he and his lab sent positive intentions, prayers, and thoughts to and they were photographed as having beautiful crystalline and filigree shapes. A third set he and his lab team sent negative thoughts too and that group's pictures revealed sharp, serrated, and irregular images. (He has another version using rice.)

Through my own research and experimentation I can say that thoughts and intentions can directly impact our physical world. The 'lighter' the things are, the easier it is to impact them. For instance, trying to cleave a rock with your mind might be a task that you can't complete in your lifetime as it is a very dense and slow substance. However, lights, radio waves, thoughts, emotions, phone calls are on the other end of the spectrum. These are naturally very 'light.'

Want some proof and clear understanding that you can

affect the world with your thoughts? Try the following experiment in Watch Our Woo!

Watch Out Woo Exercise:

As I mentioned before, it is much easier to impact things or actions that are lighter. You are going to prove it to yourself. Everyday, for one week, mentally ask each traffic light you approach to 'stay green' or 'change to green.' Keep repeating this until you are through it and then express gratitude. Notice the difference in your thoughts, energy, intentions, emotions when you conduct your traffic light experiment.

PLEASE: Always practice safe driving, or being a non-distracting passenger for your driver. I have found that mental requests work fine. It's not necessary to ask out loud in order to change the world. You can do it with your thoughts.

Did it work? Maybe the 2nd or 3rd time?

_____

_____

_____

Eventually this will become second nature and you can sail across town hitting a magical run of green lights. Sounds amazing, right? But what does it have to do with happiness? I am illustrating how powerful our thoughts and intentions are in actually impacting your world. Some of the, "yes but" arguments I hear in my workshops have to do with how powerless people are, or how thoughts aren't real. I have heard the question, 'Yes, but thoughts aren't real. Aren't you just asking us to trick ourselves into a better frame of mind? How is that legit?"

This is such a big misconception (one that I used to share) that I wanted to address it head on. Only believing in physical things with an apparatus big enough to see is extremely limiting and is a thought pattern only dating back to the 1700s. I am excited to see us moving to a more holistic and expansive path.

Unfortunately driving under these exciting circumstances can be distracting at first and this is why the experiment is best conducted as a passenger to start.

I want you to pay attention to what's going on inside of you while doing this exercise. It will give you some great insight. What did you notice about how you felt while doing this exercise?

_____

_____

_____

When were you most effective at this?

_____

_____

_____

In the course of developing this Traffic Light Experiment, I have had people request other types of exercises. One woman said she would have to travel 30 miles to find a traffic light! She even sent me a google map to show how isolated she was and she lived in Illinois!

Just in case you don't have any traffic lights nearby, here are two other exercises to show you how incredibly powerful you are and will help you develop your intuitive muscles. It also opens the space for what is possible, allows hope and play and fun into your daily mix.

1. *Phone a friend: all you need is 5 minutes, twice a day. Think about someone you care about that you don't talk to a lot. Mentally send them love, give them a hug, and ask them to call you. Keep it up for a week. Also, if you get the 'urge' to call other people, please do! Ask them if they were thinking of you! Report back:*

_____

_____

_____

2. *This one might be trickier. You will need a radio that can pick up a radio station clearly. Part one: Try walking past it while thinking about your chores, picking the kids up, shopping list... all the minutia we constantly have floating around in our brains. Was there*

a change in the radio output? (If there was, recruit someone else to walk by it to see if they also affect it.) Part 2: consciously think about increasing your energy and blocking the signal to the radio. BELIEVE that you are impermeable, a wall, a vast force that stops the signal from reaching the paltry little receptor. What happened?

_____

_____

_____

Try this for a week and see what results you get.

The point of sharing these woo-woo exercises is to show you and prove to you how powerful you, your thoughts, your intentions, your emotions, and your energy, actually are.

Do you feel more powerful? More magical? A little more in-control of what you can affect? Make some notes here.

_____

_____

_____

Releasing Blocks Round 2

The perpetual process of awareness-acceptance-forgiveness-understanding isn't something you do just once. It is a continuous spiral - one with no beginning and no end. Once you have truly gained understanding on a specific topic or issue that you've worked to heal, you journey on through life until you hit another moment of awareness. That brings up the opportunity for you to work through the next steps of acceptance, forgiveness, understanding, and repeat again and again through life. Each time you work through these four steps, you are making movements towards your happiness. You are an ever-evolving, ever-learning, ever-growing organic being. Isn't that exciting?! I think that the fact that we are all an ongoing work-in-progress is an expansive and ever-dynamic view of life. You are not a fixed thing, but continually dynamic and changing. You have the possibility and opportunity to consciously create your life.

With the upward spiral idea in mind, I'd like us to revisit several of our exercises. Hopefully you are a different person than when you started this book. You have now explored your insides, dug through significant chunks of your past, and released baggage you might not even have known you were carrying!

You have now seen with your own eyes and ears that your thoughts and intentions are powerful. Let's maximize your happiness game with that same focus and energy. Let's take this higher, more empowered energy state and immediately step into revisiting a releasing exercise below. I think you will find the process even more empowering and healing with your new awareness and tools.

What is a limiting thought that you are carrying around? Write out the negative thought, belief or fear here. Get some clarity on what's coming up for you.

_____

_____

_____

Using your new acceptance skills, can you identify where did this thought or belief come from?

_____

_____

_____

What forgiveness needs to happen around this negative thought, belief or fear?

_____

_____

_____

The script I have provided below for this release exercise is something I have been tweaking for a while. I've used it both on myself, and my clients, and it is the most complete way I have found to release low energy thoughts. The key component is to fill in the blanks below from your emotions rather than your mind. Don't use your head to think about what the answer should be. Rather use your heart and emotions to answer with how it feels to you instead. I've given you some starter words for each blank space, but use the right word for yourself. Its most important here that you fill in each blank with what it feels like specifically for you.

"I release this _____ (grudge, contract, negative emotion) and
take back my _____ (power, energy, happiness, freedom).

I am claiming back the energy that I was using to hold this in my space.

I chose to use this newly freed energy for _____ (health, love, passion, creativity, play) instead so I can _____ (get specific on the action).

So let it be."

Say it to yourself three times, with emphasis and like you mean it.

Do another on your own:

1. What is the limiting thought you want to release?

_____

_____

_____

2. I release this _____(grudge/negative emotion/ terrible view of myself, etc) and take back my _____ (power, energy, happiness, joy, etc)! I am claiming back my energy that I was using to hold _____ in my space. I chose to use this now-free energy for _____ (health, love, play, creativity, purpose) so that I can _____.

3. Say this to yourself three times, with emphasis and conviction.

And another?

_____

_____

_____

It might take several tries to release an old belief. That is ok and, is normal. My personal theory is that we lodge trauma in more than one location. So each time we get a chance to clear things out, that is great news!! Don't get discouraged if it comes up a few more times. Keep working to shed layers, and keep focused on how good it will feel to be clean, healed and happy.

Watch Out Woo:

Can you let yourself marvel in the power that you have within you? It is my personal belief that trauma, blocks, fibs, lies, or negative thoughts are held scattered throughout the body. It would make sense that holding this within ourselves must use some of our allotted energy. Is it any wonder we have a hard time truly using our power? We are using it, for daily and mundane survival, rather than what else we might be capable of. Can you imagine what your life could be like without carrying around all those battery suckers?

One of my favorite techniques I use for my clients is called the 'Why Game.' I don't believe I am the original creator of this self-discovery method, but I have added my own twist to it. I wanted to include this in the understanding section because this truly is a powerhouse of transformation. This one technique, if used consciously, will open your life and give you some of your deepest answers. Keep this one close and use it often.

The Why? Game

My Why Game is the easiest way to get to the bottom of something that is keeping you stuck, anxious, stressed, or confused. By playing the Why Game you are circling in on the root cause. Be like a child, persistent, open, and questioning. I call it a game so that you can approach this in an open, fun, curious way (rather than any possible linear, judging, impatient adult modus operandi that may pop up.)

Keep asking and hold yourself in the Why? space until you have a single, visceral answer. Ask why, over and over, again and again until you get a final answer that feels true.

Don't stop at 'because...' or allow yourself to feel defensive.

Why? Make it a game.

Why am I having a hard time marketing my book? Because I don't want to.

Why? Because it feels hard. And I don't want to.

Why? Because it isn't easy. Why? Because I don't feel like I know what I am doing.

Why does that matter? Because I am afraid of looking stupid.

See how me being afraid of looking stupid is the root cause? It is simple. And where I feel vulnerable, like a playground taunt (mentioned before), and is the actual block. I always feel like the root cause, when you get it, stings a little. It definitely hits close to home or you wanna say, 'ouch.'

Most root causes are blocks or assumptions that we have accepted as truth, at some point in our life.

Your turn to play! Where are you feeling blocked in your life? Do your own Why Game.

_____

_____

_____

The point of the next exercise is to clear limitations, set vast intentions and more exciting possibilities. By allowing your imagination to roam free and give yourself permission to daydream, to play with possibilities, and have fun, you are setting yourself up to be a happier person. It is so much lighter.

This is about shifting your mindset. And although it doesn't feel like it sometimes, it is just about always possible to shift how you feel. So the next time a downer thought pops into your awareness, you'll have at least two techniques to directly get back to seeing more possibility. Those downer thoughts can keep us stuck. Essentially, you will be trading in a downer thought that is limiting, with low-energy and feels like a dead end, for something that is exciting, inspiring, open, positive, and full of possibilities. And doesn't that just sound like a better place to be?

This exercise works by turning the low-energy thought

into a What IF? A possibility. Use your amazing energy to hold it, trace it, and release the underlying block. Notice your thought, and ask 'what if' questions around it. Allow yourself to play with the possibilities. Let this be a game. You never know what new ideas will come.

The What If? Game

What if whatever you want most is possible?

What if you gave yourself the permission to believe your daydreams can be reality?

What if I...?

What if my ….?

What if ...?

What if… What if anything... everything... that pops into your head could be possible?

What then?

It is so stinkin easy to doubt, to be overly cynical, to allow all the naysayers into our brain, and then start to believe in those false limitations. Hell, sometimes we even internalize that crap to the level that it becomes automatic. In response to some cool, expansive idea, we automatically shoot it down by thinking it is not possible, or we aren't enough to get it done. Amazing isn't it? So why not spend that same amount of energy in going higher, rather than lower, in terms of possibility and energetic intention.

Embody Your New Empowered Thought

Here is the second part of the What If? exercise: Believe this new empowered thought or idea for a certain amount of time, so give yourself an easy way out. Say you only stay in this thought pattern for 5 minutes or 10 minutes. Remember that whole big section on congruence? Well, it can be difficult to go from swirling around a bowl and feeling almost flushed to stepping into a realm of exciting possibilities. It can be confusing to step from upset and frustrated to happier and lighter in one go. So give yourself a time limit. Make it easy on you.

Tell yourself: Just for this day, or until lunch, or just this hour, or even these 10 minutes, I am going to allow myself to believe my big What If statement.

Then honor that pledge by spending your allotted time in that belief. If you need an even bigger crutch, you can always tell yourself, "Tomorrow (or after lunch, or at 11am or in 20 minutes) I can go back to my old beliefs, but, right now, for the next 10 minutes I'll fully examine this possibility." Give your What If some air time. Give your happiness airtime.

What is something that you would like to explore for yourself in life? What have you been mulling over and then running away from? Have you had the beginning of a thought like, "I wonder what would happen if I…" and then immediately you canned it? Or, "Wow, it would be really cool if I could…" What is one of these these statements that you have never allowed yourself to explore?

_____

_____

_____

I did one, so you can see what this might look like. :

I'd really like to write a book. But… no one will…what if… what if someone did read it? What if a lot of people read it?

I gave myself 20 minutes to believe that I wrote a book, and that people loved to read it. Then, I checked in to see how it felt without judgement and wrote about what came up. What if I wrote a book? What if people read it? What if it helped a lot of people? What if I became known as an author and a researcher for holistic wellness? What if I could help the alternative health movement gain validity? What if

I could help others become inspired and motivated to work on themselves? What if…?

What are your What If statements?

_____

_____

_____

Important Truths

Now, using all of what we have been through together… over a 180 pages of exploring and digging and growing your happiness, let's summarize a few truths that you have discovered about yourself and about consciously creating your own happiness practice.

What adjectives describe you?

_____

_____

_____

Who are you?

_____

_____

_____

Why are you here? What is your purpose?

_____

_____

_____

What emotions make up your own personal definition of happiness?

_____

_____

_____

What gives you those feelings/emotions/thoughts?

_____

_____

_____

You have the tools now. You've been through this whole book. I want you to understand your own definition of happiness. How would you define it?

_____

_____

_____

What does it include for you? What makes up your happiness definition?

_____

_____

_____

What emotion words do you use to describe it?

_____

_____

_____

If it has a taste what is it?

_____

A scent?

Does it have a feeling?

What does it look like?

I want you to be so clearly descriptive, and intimately possessive of your happiness definition that these words and this feeling is yours and no one else's. Your goal is to have your definition of happiness be so descriptive that it can be your compass even on those days you feel most lost or upset. So, is there anything else that you want to add here to describe your happiness definition?

Wonderful!!! Good job. I am so proud of all you have accomplished and dug through.

Happiness is a practice. You've learned a lot in this book. You might get new ideas about how you want to approach your happiness, or you might want to stick with what you've created here. Whatever it is, own your happiness. Consciously create it. Being happy is not an accident, and isn't handed out on silver platters. Every happy person you know has done some work to be that way. You have to create your own and you've taken amazing strides throughout *My Happiness Handbook.*

So what's next? Practice these exercises. Support your metamorphosis into the kind of person you want to be. Look for ways to embody your happiness practice, allow yourself to fully enjoy life, and NEVER believe that you don't have the right to be happy.

Summing Up Understanding

In this last section,

1. We have explored your true power through a few exercises. We tracked the results and it was pretty exciting!
2. We revisited the idea of releasing blocks and stuck parts with another set of intentions as a more advanced exercise.
3. I shared my What If Exercise and my Why Game with you and we went through how that creates so much more space and opportunities in life!

4. We reiterated and really nailed down what your happiness practice is to you.
5. We explored happiness through your senses and firmly fixed it into your framework.

Congratulations!

Congratulations!! You have completed a huge shift in moving forward into your own happiness! You have grown your own happiness practice and completed massive mind, body, spiritual and emotional upleveling.

GOOD JOB!!

The techniques and resources I have shared in this book can be used each time you are experiencing downer thoughts, or blocks. You can work through them with what you have learned here, DIY style. Thank you for investing your time in your happiness journey. I can't think of a better place to spend such a valuable resource.

If you ever get stuck, or need just a smidge more individual attention, drop me an email or Facebook message. I am only a thought away.

Peace and blessings, light and highest happiness,
Becky

Acknowledgments

In gratitude and owing a debt of thanks that will be hard to repay in kind…

To Misti Patrella. My editor, co-conspirator, enabler, sounding board, and champion. Also, my project manager and general go-to person. Thank you for everything and sticking with me through this process. You can find out more about her and her work at http://www.mistipatrella.com

To Adam. My support team, always keeping the hearth fires burning to guide me home.

To my herd. For lending me four hooves and a strong back when my own feet can't carry me fast or far enough.

References

Archetypes

Howell, Becky. "Quit Giving Up Happiness, Part 1." YouTube, 2 Aug. 2017, youtu.be/FTgqsTtaRsA.

"Jungian Archetypes." Wikipedia, Wikimedia Foundation, 9 Apr. 2018, en.wikipedia.org/wiki/Jungian_archetypes.

Myss, Caroline. "Appendix: A Gallery of Archetypes." Caroline Myss, www.myss.com/free-resources/sacred-contracts-and-your-archetypes/appendix-a-gallery-of-archtypes/.

Cartesian Reductionist Theory

"Cartesian Reductionism." Hmolpedia, www.eoht.info/page/Cartesian+reductionism.

"Descartes and the Cartesian Dogma of a Mechanical Universe." FUTURE SCHOOL, www.holisticeducator.com/descartes.htm#Cartesian doctrine.

Aron, Arthur. "Questions Psychologists Says Will Make Anyone Fall in Love." Idea Pod. https://ideapod.com/questions-psychologist-says-will-make-fall-love-anyone/?utm_source=facebook&utm_medium=link&utm_campaign=js

Borelli, Lizette. "Why Do We Cry?" Medical Daily. http://www.medicaldaily.com/pulse/why-do-we-cry-three-different-types-tears-and-their-physiology-331708

Crystal, Billy, Carrie Fisher, Meg Ryan, Rob Reiner, and Bruno Kirby. 2011. *When Harry Met Sally*. Santa Monica, Calif: MGM Studio distributed by Twentieth Century Fox Home Entertainment.

"Etymology of the Word 'Forgive.'" Stack Exchange. https://english.stackexchange.com/questions/343990/etymology-of-word-forgive

Explore (NY). 2006 Sep-Oct;2(5):408-11.

Double-blind test of the effects of distant intention on water crystal formation.

Greenberg, Leslie S., and Sandra C. Paivio. Working with Emotions in Psychotherapy. Guilford Press, 2003.

Hartley, Gemma. "Women Aren't Nags-We're Just Fed Up." Harper's BAZAAR, Harper's BAZAAR, 9 Oct. 2017, www.harpersbazaar.com/culture/features/a12063822/emotional-labor-gender-equality/.

"'It's so Incredible to Finally Be Understood.'" 16Personalities, www.16personalities.com/.

Lamott, Anne. https://www.facebook.com/AnneLamott/posts/593723490757298

Markegard, Doniga. Dawn Again: Tracking the Wisdom of the Wild. Georgetown Publications Incorporated, 2017.

McLeod, Saul. "Stress and Life Events." Simply Psychology. https://www.simplypsychology.org/SRRS.html

Merriam-Webster Dictionary, Online edition, s.v. "holistic", https://www.merriam-webster.com/dictionary/holistic

Pert, Candace B. Molecules of Emotion: Why You Feel the Way You Feel. Pocket Books, 1999.

Prochaska & DiClemente, 1983, *Transtheoretical Model of Behavioral Change*.

Reinhardt, Michelle, 2017. *Hack Your Happiness Podcast:* Mindset Energy and Healing Transformations

http://michellereinhardt.com.au/hack-your-happiness-for-unlimited-abundance-with-becky-howell/

"Releasing the Role of Emotional Caretaker." Womb of Light, www.womboflight.com/releasing-the-role-of-emotional-caretaker/.

Ruiz, Miguel. 1997. *The four agreements: a practical guide to personal freedom*. San Rafael, Calif: Amber-Allen Pub.

San Francisco, Psyched in. "Emotional Labor Takes a Toll on Women." The Huffington Post, TheHuffingtonPost.com, 7 Dec. 2017,

SparkNotes Editors. "SparkNote on Principles of Philosophy." SparkNotes.com. SparkNotes LLC. n.d.. Web. 24 Jan. 2018.

Timberg, Scott. Here Are My Thoughts on Forgiveness, Trust Me on This Series, 12/2/14.

"Virtues List." Virtuesforlife.com, www.virtuesforlife.com/virtues-list/.

What If Game

Howell, Becky E. "What If Game." January 2016. Coaching resource.

The Why Game

Howell, Becky E. 'The Why Game." January 2016. Coaching resource.

Wilson, James & Kelling, George. Atlantic Monthly. *"Broken Windows: Police and Neighborhood Change."* 1969.

Additional Support

Even though I have done my best to make this a stand alone book and as complete as possible, a book does have some limitations. Here are a couple of other ways for you to continue this work If you want or need more support and guidance for finding your happiness.

Online Workshop

I periodically offer an online class called My Happiness Masterclass. This is where we bring the material in this book to life. It is a deep dive into your happiness. The benefit here is that there is plenty of space to ask questions, and hear how others are working through the material.

In-Person Workshop

If you are looking to hang out in-person, I also run How to Be Happier Workshops. These are a blast and so much fun! We focus here on bringing more happiness into your life, group, or organization. If you would like to schedule one of these for your group, we might be able to make that happen!

Equine Facilitated Healing Experiences

Finally, I am incredibly blessed to facilitate Equine Facilitated Healing Experiences. These are individual, in-person only experience designed to guide you towards deep healing around a situation. I find that they transport you to a different plain of energy, intention, presence, and action.

More information for any of my services can be found at both www.beckyhowell.com and www.myhappinesspractice.com. Please feel free to send me an email with your particulars to info@myhappinesspractice.com.

About The Author

Becky Howell is a long-time multipreneur in the Health and Wellness Industry and is constantly searching for holistic ways to help others be happy, healthy, and sustainable. She is an author, consultant and coach, speaker, and workshop facilitator on a global scale.

My Happiness Handbook is Becky's second book in the

series and is now being incorporated into her *How to Be Happier* workshops. Don't forget to check out *My Happiness Masterclass* (an online class that brings this book to life). If you would like more information on these events, please check her website.

New endeavors include diving deep into Therapeutic Herbalism, learning about electromagnetic and photonic therapies, swimming with large pinnipeds, and working on her third book.

You can find Becky online at:

LinkedIn: https://www.linkedin.com/in/becky-howellcoach/

Facebook: https://www.facebook.com/BeckyHowell-HappinessExpert/

Website: https://www.beckyhowell.com/

https://www.myhappinesspractice.com/

www.ingramcontent.com/pod-product-compliance
Lightning Source LLC
Chambersburg PA
CBHW071204070526
44584CB00019B/2908